Roger Dyson, a qualified teacher, General Council and Register o background of nutrition and natu at the College of Homœopathy, registered member of the Society of Homœopaths and Fellow of the Register of Herbalists, he lectures at various colleges and holds seminars around the world.

This is his second book, following Classical Homœopathy Revisited, co-written with Jean Cole, published in England in 1997, which was well received in many countries.

He pioneered Diagnostic Kinesiology, which he teaches in regular workshops and seminars, and much of this book includes the results of his experiences. He practises in the towns of Reykjavik and Akureyri in Iceland, and at Newlands Park Health Care Centre, South London.

Rona Francis graduated from Sheffield University with a degree in Physiology in 1993. She is a qualified teacher and studied Homeopathy at the London College of Classical Homœopathy graduating in 2000. She is a member of the Alliance of Registered Homœopaths and has been working alongside Roger Dyson since 2004, using and developing Diagnostic Kinesiology at Newlands Park Natural Health Care Centre.

She holds regular workshops on diagnostic kinesiology and has lectured in several countries on nutrition and health related issues. She has previously been published in Homeopathy In Practice relating to her work when dealing with electricity and geopathic stress. She is currently expanding her practice with the development and use of Bioresonance.

Jóna Ágústa Ragnheiðardóttir is a member of the Society of Homeopaths in Iceland. She graduated from the College of Homœopathy in 2000; her final thesis being: *"Maintaining Causes – Hahneman's paragraph 259-261 revisited and brought up to date"*. Her contribution to this book is based on that thesis and further studies in the field.

She worked with Roger Dyson at Newlands Park Natural Health Care Centre in London where she finished a course in Applied Kinesiology and has lectured at Roger Dyson's seminars in London. Jóna is also a qualified Reflexologist and a member of the Society of Reflexologists in Iceland. She is now a practising homœopath in Reykjavik, Iceland tel: 00354 895 3836. email: homopati@simnet.is.

Obtaining Optimum Health

OR

Why your illness is not getting better
and what you can do about it.

A handbook for practitioners, their patients and the public. A little book which can make a big difference to your health.

by
Roger Dyson,
Rona Francis
and Jóna Ágústa Ragnheiðardóttir

Winter Press
16 Stambourne Way
West Wickham
Kent BR4 9NF
e-mail: ooh@winterpress.net

First published by Winter Press in 2009
Reprinted 2011

ISBN 9781 874581 093 r1

Cover design by Colin Winter
Printed by Goodnews Press, Essex, UK

CONTENTS

ACKNOWLEDGEMENT

Our thanks to Paul Burnett for his proof-reading, as well as for supplying some interesting and valuable additional ideas. Paul is an experienced Homœopath and Kinesiologist from West Wickham in Kent who also enjoys editing books on Alternative Health, and he has put his full weight behind this project.

CONTACTING THE AUTHORS

The authors will be pleased to hear from you via any of the following:

Newlands Park Healthcare Centre,
48 Newlands Park,
London SE26 5NE
t: 020 8659 5001
e: dropbox@traditional-health.co.uk
www.traditional-health.co.uk
www.allergytestinglondon.co.uk

FOREWORD

There are many books available that suggest one cure for all illnesses or for one category of illness. In general these offer a very simplified view of human disease. While these sorts of books can raise the hopes of the general public and practitioners, and offer some useful insights for some people, they do not usually deliver on their promise.

In this book Roger, Rona and Jóna outline a more complex understanding of ill health. They place an emphasis throughout the book on the importance of people being viewed as individuals, with their own unique combination of disturbances. They see that often several factors come together, and that these all need to be addressed in order to return the person to a state of health. They show how the maintaining causes will be different for each person, not each condition. This echoes my own findings from over twenty years of using kinesiology with people suffering a wide range of health problems. There are frequently occurring factors, and many of these are discussed here, but there are no hard and fast rules about what factors relate to which conditions. They also recognise that there may not be one cause. Instead there is often an interplay between different factors, with each one varying in its importance at any time. Finding and correcting these different factors is both fascinating and rewarding.

Roger, Rona and Jóna have written a book filled with information and research on maintaining causes. They include many interesting case histories to highlight particular points. I hope that like me you will find this book fascinating to read.

Jane Thurnell-Read

PREFACE

In the first two paragraphs of his work *The Organon,* Samuel Hahnemann says that the physician's highest and only mission is to restore the sick to health in the shortest, most reliable and most harmless way. In his third paragraph he stresses that the physician must clearly perceive what is to be cured in diseases. He must know the obstacles to recovery in each case and how to remove them. *"Then he understands how to treat judiciously and rationally, and he is a true practitioner of the healing art"*[1].

These statements from the father of homœopathy are still valid and should be written in the heart of every practitioner. In some cases the obstacles to cure are obvious, such as the use of medication or recreational drugs, unhealthy living conditions etc. In other cases however, the obstacles to cure remain hidden, e.g. the influence of environmental pollution, food intolerances, the ill effects of amalgam fillings, or a reaction to electrical devices. Practitioners often find themselves effecting superficial cures for ailments, only to find the patient re-presenting with another outer aspect of their inner disease a few months later.

1 'Organon of Medicine', Samuel Hahnemann, pp.92-93

Dealing with such maintaining causes forces the practitioner to return to fundamentals to root out the underlying problem. Discovering the maintaining causes has always been a difficult and demanding process. In his book *'The Principles and Art of Cure by Homœopathy'*, Herbert A. Roberts said that unfortunately in his time there were no instruments of precision by which to measure the obstacles to the curative waves of the remedies. Nowadays there are instruments that can assist practitioners in their search for maintaining causes. The authors use diagnostic kinesiology, as described in Chapter 4. There are also popular electronic devices, such as bioresonance machines, which may provide the practitioner with a lot of information, but still the simple underlying cause is not always identified. If the root of the problem can be tracked down by ways described in this book and simple remedial action put into place, then the body is able to heal itself in a way which would not be possible just by the use of medicines, either natural or chemical.

CHAPTER 1

SETTING THE SCENE – CAUSATION OF DISEASE

An increasing number of books are rolling off the presses and filling the shelves in health food shops, full of self-help tips about various problems, and newly-discovered or rediscovered remedies for different ailments. So why are we adding to this situation? What makes this book different?

We are not giving a general herbal or nutritional recipe that will cure a particular condition for all patients. Many suggested prescriptions will improve and alleviate these conditions, but the complete cure can often seem elusive to practitioner and patient. The reason for this is simple. The causes of arthritis and other ailments will vary for different people and, unless this individuality is addressed, a complete and lasting cure will often escape even the best health practitioner.

Orthodox medicine, with its use of chemical drugs, has few answers either. The drugs may palliate and relieve symptoms, but many patients soon return to their former state when they stop taking the prescribed medicine. The double-blind trial, where sufferers of a condition are given either drugs or a placebo and their progress is then monitored, gives us statistical information about the clinical response of a particular group of people. However this only measures the progress while they continue to take the medicine. Once the double-blind trial ceases and people are no longer taking the drugs, or in some instances no longer benefiting from the psychological boost of the placebo, the symptoms will return to their original state. Nothing has dealt with the root cause.

Acute disease provides us with a different situation. Acute disease is self-limiting, which means that a person will recover or die from his condition. There is nothing to maintain an ongoing state of illness, and when germs/pathogens are killed by strong drugs, or when the immune system is boosted by certain health regimes, then the body is able to fight back and regain health. If a swab is taken of the average person's throat, streptococcus bacteria are often found – this does not however mean that everyone has a streptococcus throat infection. The streptococcus bacteria only become pathogenic if the immune system is lowered because of stress, a chill, poor nutrition or other factors. After two or three weeks the sore throat will usually be better, with or without any treatment; however if, six months later, it is still posing a problem, we know that there is a maintaining cause. There is something that allows the bacteria to continue to adversely affect the sufferer, and it is vital to discover what this is if we are to obtain a satisfactory resolution and cure.

Our own training includes a background of herbal medicine, naturopathy, homœopathy and kinesiology. A homœopath, Pritam Singh, was a considerable influence for us and his ideas led us to re-evaluate some of the writings of Samuel Hahnemann, founder of modern-day homœopathy over two hundred years ago, and to examine their relevance for the present day. The result of this was the book *"Classical Homœopathy Revisited"* by Jean Cole and Roger Dyson, published by Winter Press. This book discussed some of the best ways to stimulate the body to heal itself. The principles and methodologies discussed in the book produced a significantly greater rate of both cure and improvement. Judging by the encouraging postbag, they also helped many other homœopathic practitioners and students.

However it must be said that there were some patients without serious pathology who were still not progressing at the rate for which we would have hoped and this led us to continue our research. As a result we discovered how the 'old pioneers' of homœopathy emphasised the necessity of dealing with that which sustains the disease and means that the patient will continue to suffer, i.e. the maintaining causes of disease. If these were not addressed, it would be as if we were forever bailing out a boat with a hole in the bottom, no matter what medicine was employed.

As another analogy: there is little point in putting cream on a mosquito bite if, subsequently, windows and doors are left open for more mosquitoes to enter and attack. Killing the mosquito and closing doors and windows does not however bring immediate relief: patience is required, but the soothing cream can now begin to take effect.

Much health treatment today, both orthodox and unorthodox, mainstream, complementary and alternative, is like the soothing cream and of limited benefit unless those doors and windows are shut. In other words, our bodies' internal environment needs to be such that bacteria, viruses, parasites and fungi are no longer pathogenic and causing problems. Unless the maintaining cause is addressed from the outset, people may either rail at orthodox medicine or complain that complementary or alternative treatments are not effective.

Once we start to deal with the fundamental causes of illness, we can discover and remove some of the important toxic load which is afflicting the individual. Medicines can now assist with cure rather than with palliation. Chemical drugs may have a much more limited role. For instance, those for pain relief and inflammation will largely become redundant as the situation improves. The only essential drugs will be those giving the body raw materials, such as thyroxine, adrenaline and insulin, which, if the relevant organs and glands have been damaged, the body is incapable of producing by itself.

CHAPTER 2

THE SCENE OVER 200 YEARS AGO

Samuel Hahnemann, a doctor and naturopath and the pioneer of modern-day homœopathy, who lived over 200 years ago, wrote a book on medical practice, '*Organon of Medicine*', which appeared in various editions between 1810 and 1833. In many ways this book was far ahead of its time and many of the principles laid down in it are still very relevant today. It begins,

> *"The physician's high and only mission is to restore the sick to health, to cure, as it is termed. The highest ideal of cure is rapid, gentle and permanent restoration of health, or removal and annihilation of the disease in its whole extent, in the shortest, most reliable and most harmless way, on easily comprehensible principles."*

Much of the book continues with information regarding the mode of employing medicines until, in paragraph 259 and following, he writes that during any treatment, everything which could be a hindrance must be removed from the diet and lifestyle. He continues:

> *"Hence the careful investigation into such obstacles to cure is so much the more necessary in the case of patients affected by chronic diseases, as their diseases are usually aggravated by such noxious influences and other disease-causing errors in the diet and regimen, which often pass unnoticed".*

The "obstacles to cure" will be different for each patient, rather than for each condition. Because of our inherited constitutions and individual susceptibilities, what is a pollutant for one patient may be easily tolerated or even beneficial to another. This is why many drugs and medicines only palliate and why much research is limited in its usefulness. More research techniques are now being devised to uncover these maintaining causes, and by careful discussion and case study we can correctly identify them in our patients.

As acute disease is, by definition, self-limiting, Samuel Hahnemann confines his comments to chronic or long-standing conditions, for which he makes these recommendations:

> *"The most appropriate regimen, during the employment of medicine in chronic diseases, consists in the removal of such obstacles to recovery and in supplying where necessary the reverse: innocent moral and intellectual recreation, active exercise in the open air in almost all kinds of weather (daily walks, slight manual labour), suitable, nutritious unmedicinal food and drink".*

Some of the examples of things to avoid given in his footnote seem quaint nowadays, and not all would we ourselves recommend, but many of the principles are still valid. His list of things to be avoided reads thus:

> *"Coffee; fine Chinese and other herb teas; beer prepared with medicinal vegetable substances unsuitable for the patient's state; so-called fine liquors made with medicinal spices; all kinds of punch; spiced chocolate; odorous waters and perfumes of many kinds; strong-scented flowers in the apartment; tooth powders and essences and perfumed sachets compounded of drugs; highly spiced dishes and sauces; spiced cakes and ices; crude medicinal vegetables for soups; dishes of herbs, roots and stalks of plants possessing medicinal qualities; old cheese, and meats that are in a state of decomposition, or that possess medicinal properties (as the flesh and fat of pork, ducks and geese, or veal that is too young and sour viands), ought just as certainly to be kept from patients as they should avoid all excesses in food and in the use of sugar and salt; as also spirituous drinks, 'undiluted with water'; heated rooms, woollen clothing next to the skin (which should be exchanged in warm weather, first for cotton, then for linen garments); a sedentary life in close apartments; or the frequent indulgence in mere passive exercise (such as riding, driving or swinging); pro-*

longed suckling; taking a long siesta in a recumbent posture (in bed); sitting up long at night; uncleanliness; unnatural debauchery; enervation by reading obscene books, [reading while lying down, Onanism or imperfect or suppressed intercourse in order to prevent conception]; subjects of anger, grief or vexation; a passion for play; over-exertion of mind or body; dwelling in marshy districts; damp rooms; penurious living, &c. All these things must be as far as possible avoided or removed, in order that the cure may not be obstructed or rendered impossible. Some of my disciples seem needlessly to increase the difficulties of the patient's dietary by forbidding the use of many more, tolerably indifferent things, which is not to be commended".

In order to find both the causes and cure of illnesses Hahnemann studied lifestyles, negative environmental influences, hygiene, diet and regimen. He recommended the avoidance of certain substances and stimulants in food and drink that could act medicinally, such as coffee, tea, certain vegetables, highly spiced foods, etc. He also suggested that woollen clothing, heated damp rooms and a sedentary life in airless rooms should be avoided too. Hahnemann ascribes the following chronic disorders to the use of coffee:

"constipation, impotence, dental caries, abscesses in children, pulmonary mucus, blue rings around the eyes, leucorrhoea, ulcers, general megrim, nervous affections, chronic diseases, insomnia, stammering of speech, lack of appetite for food, ophthalmias and rattling in the chest".[1]

Although much time has passed since Hahnemann made his observations, the essence of his writing is still valid. We mostly consume the same items that he mentions, but modern diets are more refined and diverse than in his time. As Dr Hulda Clark states,

"We have coffee-blend with various tastes, decaffeinated coffee, a whole range of fruit juice, soda pop, herb tea

1 Hahnemann pp401-9, 'On the effects of coffee from original observations, lesser writings' Leipzig 1803

blends, carbonated drinks and beverages with Nutrasweet, which are all contaminated with solvents left over from the manufacturing process".[2]

We are also in contact with an increasing number of chemicals in our everyday life. It is those with which we are in continual contact that can affect us. For instance, Hahnemann wrote about "perfumes of many kinds". We have recently seen irritable bowel syndrome resolve itself with one man who stopped using aftershave, and a woman's breathing problem subsided after she changed her perfume. It is sometimes profitable to ask oneself "what new products have I started to use shortly before this condition began?".

When Hahnemann wrote about attention to regimen he was not only conscious about what to avoid, but also of giving the patient healthy raw materials. In his later work, entitled 'Chronic Diseases', he states that before the use of medicines it is necessary to remove that which is hurtful and to put patients on a nourishing and strengthening diet. A lack of nutritious food and water is responsible for far more health problems than is commonly realised.

CHAPTER 3

THE 21ST CENTURY REVISITED

Today we often find that pollutants such as metals and electromagnetic stress, or just being chronically dehydrated, can adversely effect our health. One of the problems is that these factors make us more susceptible to other unnatural substances found in our food and environment. Our bodies can cope with and filter out a degree of toxicity. However, there's always something that is the proverbial final straw to break the camel's back. Our

2 Clark p.428, 'The Cure for all Diseases', New Century Press, Chula Vista, USA 1995

experience shows that by dealing with electromagnetic stress, metals and dehydration, our bodies are able to cope better with chemicals in foods and do not produce the same allergic reactions. Perhaps if we did not have the chemicals in foods, our bodies would deal better with metals, but we need to take the easiest option to regain our health.

Within the last few decades our lives have changed rapidly in almost every aspect; the environment, the air that we breathe, the food we eat, the water we drink, all of these contain different kinds of toxicity which our bodies must cope with. The list of diseases produced by man-made toxins must be expanded to include those caused by the thousands of potentially harmful chemicals released into our environment. Chemicals are used out in the fields in the form of fertilisers and insecticides. Livestock is fed on manufactured food containing additives – which include antibiotics, synthetic vitamins and minerals, and hormones. In order to prolong the shelf-life of products and improve their appearance we use chemicals, colourings, and preservatives, and then we wrap them up in plastic and aluminium. Finally, we cook our food in pots and pans made of aluminium. In his book, 'Elements of Homœopathy', Sankaran quotes Grimmer,

> *"...and most important of all the patient must refrain from food prepared and cooked in aluminium ware and its alloys"*[3].

In dealing with maintaining causes, it is very useful to have knowledge of the main pollutants we are dealing with (see Appendix 1).

The Canadian physicist and microbiologist, Dr Hulda Clark, who for decades has done research into toxicity, came to the conclusion that mineral water has solvents in it from machinery and sterilising equipment used in the bottling process. She states that this water is stagnant and is soon contaminated with our own bacteria from

3 'Elements of Homœopathy', Vol. 2, Rajan Sankaran, p.526

contact with mouth or hands. Staphylococcus and E-coli are commonly seen in mineral water. She recommends that we drink tap water only. Although it may have 500 toxic elements in it, she says that it is less likely to contain solvents in detectable amounts. She says that filters trap pollutants and allow tiny amounts to enter the water on a daily basis. Her opinion is that such chronic toxin consumption is much worse for the health than periodic surges of toxins and she recommends the use of a small filter that is changed every month to reduce the risk. This can de-chlorinate the water and improve the flavour.

These are just some brief examples of the effect of civilisation on our environment, and especially on our nutritional intake. However, we have to live in the real world and we are not advocating a fanatical approach or turning our back on modern living and the twenty-first century. If our energy and health is good, and if healthy complementary treatment is given, our bodies have a great ability to detoxify themselves and reduce susceptibility to a minimum.

A toxic internal environment, as a result of chemical pollutants previously mentioned, will upset the body's homeostasis and can produce the environment in which pathological bacteria can flourish, or which causes benign bacteria to become pathological. Hahnemann was aware of the problems of invasive organisms and this led him to formulate his views on scabies and psora (Hahnemann's term for a general under-functioning of the metabolism). However, 200 years ago, he had little ability to differentiate between micro-organisms.

Hahnemann, who was far ahead of his time, knew that disease forming parasites and toxins derange the vital force or natural restorative energy of the body, making it very hard to cure degenerative chronic diseases. He used the term 'acquired miasm' for infection by micro-organisms:

> *"It includes symptoms transmitted to following generations, because such miasms produce auto-immune and immuno-deficiency disorders, in which the organism attacks its own healthy tissue, while masking the mutation of cells from the defence system. The effects of these disorders are passed through the generations producing more complex forms of inherited chronic miasms whose symptoms manifest as hundreds of disease names in modern pathology."*
>
> *'What are Miasms?' David Little*

Doctors and health practitioners are becoming aware of the widespread problem of parasites and bacteria in the human system, and their role in major and minor health challenges. They are increasingly recognising the importance of the gastro-intestinal tract in the development of auto-immune disease. Diseases in this category include lupus, alopecia, rheumatoid arthritis, polymyalgia rheumatica, multiple sclerosis, fibromyalgia, chronic fatigue syndrome, Sjogren's syndrome, vitiligo, thyroiditis, vasculitis, Crohn's disease, ulcerative colitis, urticaria (hives), diabetes and Raynaud's disease[4]. Over the past few years, microbiologists have found and labelled some 50 new gut bacteria[5].

The cause of 'leaky gut syndrome' is inflammation of the gut lining, which can be brought about by various factors. The gut becomes leaky in the sense that bacteria, fungi, and parasites, plus their toxins, normally not absorbed into the bloodstream in the healthy state, pass through a damaged, hyper-permeable intestinal lining. In healthier circumstances the toxic material would be repelled and eliminated. The leaky gut syndrome is almost always associated with auto-immune disease, and reversing auto-immune disease depends on healing the lining of the gastro-intestinal tract.

The inflammation that causes the leaky gut syndrome also damages the protective coating of the IgA family

4 'Leaky Gut Syndrome', Good Health Guides, Elizabeth Lipski

5 The Times, 25th April 2000

(Immunoglobin A), normally present in a healthy gut. Since IgA helps us ward off infections, with leaky gut problems we are less resistant to viruses, bacteria, parasites and candida. These microbes are then able to invade the bloodstream and colonise almost any body tissue or organ. These microbes and their toxins, if present in large enough amounts, can outstrip the liver's ability to detoxify. This results in symptoms such as confusion, memory loss, brain fog etc. In many cases certain pollutants in the body can attract micro-organisms.

Hulda Clark says that tapeworms usually have preferred locations and that the favourite organ for dirofilaria (dog heartworm, also found in man), is the heart. She has, however, discovered that it can live in other organs too, if they are sufficiently polluted with solvents, metals and other toxins. That is why she writes about a new kind of parasitism, based on pollution – parasites have their special targets, as do solvents[6]. An example of this is the flatworm or 'fluke's' cycle, which normally has six stages, but only the adult stage normally lives in the human, and only in the intestine. The second stage of the flatworm depends on a snail, but when the body has pollutants in it, the other five stages, i.e. the egg, miracidia, redia, cercaria and metacercaria, can develop within it. The egg is passed by human bowel movements and can find its way into areas where snails dwell. The miracidia hatches, finds a snail host and from these develop the redia and cercaria. The cercaria swims from the snail to a plant, which it may be feeding on, and here forms a cyst. As man eats the plant, so the digestive secretions break down the cyst wall and an adult flatworm emerges to live in the intestines. Up to 1000 eggs can then be produced with each bowel movement, and thus the cycle continues.

If the eggs of ascaris lumbricoides are swallowed, they settle down in the intestine and grow to adulthood.

6 'The Cure for all Diseases', p.32 and following, Dr Hulda Clark

However, they can migrate from the ailimentary tract into the blood and lymphatic system where they can then settle and weaken vulnerable organs anywhere in the body. If the larvae are numerous enough a person may have shortness of breath and lung inflammations. Hulda Clark found that ascaris is apparent in many respiratory and skin problems, including eczema, asthma and psoriasis.

Strongyloids is a hookworm living in the soil and when eaten it becomes parasitic in the bowel[7]. According to Hulda Clark these can easily travel to the brain and she claims to find them present in every case of migraine.

We can take the example of a 15-year-old girl who visited our clinic with migraines. She was found to have sensitivity to lead, cocoa, cow's milk, strongyloids and geopathic stress (see Chapter 8). Her sensitivity to geopathic stress was eliminated using the techniques described in Chapter 4 and Appendix 2. This led her to no longer being sensitive to the lead, cocoa, cow's milk and strongyloids and the migraines cleared up. This demonstrated that geopathic stress was the pollutant that was allowing the strongyloids to be a problem.

On another occasion a woman came to the clinic complaining of migraines, but Diagnostic Kinesiology revealed that strongyloids were not a factor. When asked if she had taken any drugs recently she admitted to taking narcotics following a tooth extraction. In this case it was not a true migraine, but rather the side effects of the drugs that were causing the pain; once the narcotics were ceased the migraines stopped.

To treat gastrointestinal problems correctly, treatments must include the removal of the maintaining cause and the improvement of function and healing of the gut lining. Certain food items can work at exacerbating these prob-

7 'Man, Nature & Disease', Richard Fiennes, p.99

lems. Cow's milk is usually contaminated with shigella bacteria, as well as fluke parasite stages. Pasteurisation does not kill them all – only boiling for at least half a minute makes milk safe. Shigella causes fatigue, irritability and depression (Clark, p.425). Obviously not everyone who drinks milk becomes susceptible to shigella, as normally it would just pass through the body, so it is only when the ecology, or flora, of the gut is unhealthy that the bacteria will thrive, multiply and cause functional problems.

A girl of 19 came to our clinic who, since the age of 13, had suffered from severe stomach pain that had been diagnosed by doctors firstly as abdominal migraine, and secondly as an ovarian cyst. More recently, she had been diagnosed as suffering from irritable bowel syndrome. Previously homœopathic remedies produced no improvement, except Colocynth, which helped her acute cramps. Applied Kinesiology showed that she harboured the shigella bacteria and ascaris. She also had an intolerance to cow's milk and butter and a limited tolerance to bread and wheat. Geopathic stress was also affecting her. By protecting and de-sensitising herself to geopathic stress (see chapters 4 and 8), her intolerance to the other substances was eliminated, and she took turmeric and fennel to change the environment in the intestines. At her follow-up appointment five weeks later she said that she had not felt as well for many years.

Many infants with colic have been given cow's milk products contaminated with shigella at an age when their immature stomachs couldn't handle its effect. Fennel is anti-spasmodic, but also creates an environment in the intestine incompatible with shigella. This makes it a valuable addition to many gripe waters. In a similar way, many who travel to the east and continue with a typical English diet may succumb to E. coli or shigella infections, which cause no problem to the local residents who have a diet rich in turmeric and cinnamon.

Another example is that of a 30-year-old woman who had 'flu' with bronchitis and had been taking antibiotics. Her cough had disappeared, but she felt terribly unwell: she felt blocked and had no energy. Applied Kinesiology showed that she was sensitive to cow's milk due to shigella, which brought about bloating: however she was not sensitive to boiled milk, in which the shigella had been killed. She was prescribed turmeric, fennel, some homœopathic remedies and advised to avoid unboiled milk. Four weeks later her energy had increased, she had had no bloating for over two weeks and repeat testing showed no weakness to cow's milk or shigella.

Staphylococcus is another very common bacteria and recently we saw a young girl with spots on her thighs and genital area. Her skin was also dry and she had breathing difficulties. In cold weather she would get spots on her mouth, which would last for about a week, starting as red patches before developing into spots. She had had a dry cough, which had ceased after the carpets were removed in her home. Applied Kinesiology showed weakness with staphylococcus, aluminium, chlorine, dog hair and wheat. In order to clear the staphylococcus the practitioner advised her to avoid or reduce flour, bread, pastries, use of aluminium pots and pans, swimming and soap. Sulphur, in descending potencies, was prescribed for one day, then alternate Pulsatilla 30 and Staphylococcus 30. At her return visit the mother said that everything had cleared up within a week.

Bacteria multiply in the presence of disease tissue. They are the result, not the cause, of the tissue breakdown. Yeast infection is the result of negative alteration of the intestinal environment and antibiotics are frequently responsible for this change in the gut. By restoring the internal environment, the fungus will revert to normal, benign levels. However, no discussion on the gut is complete without mentioning that amalgam fillings in teeth can leak and, in those people with sensitivity, will create a toxic environment in that area, allowing pathogenic bacteria to flourish (see Chapter 9).

Hahnemann came to the conclusion that the constitution becomes used to many things over a longer period of time. If they are not maintaining the disease, there is no reason to remove them all at once[8]. The aim is always to remove the cause of disease so that the body is unencumbered and free to heal itself.

Just as in Hahnemann's time, the modern list of things to be avoided or removed is long and we have named only a few. We are not saying that everyone must avoid all the harmful things on that list, as we have to live in the modern world and this would be impractical. If we have a good balanced diet and pay some attention to our lifestyle, then the avoidance of the substances should not be necessary. If, however, the immune system is weak and the body is suffering from a serious condition, then we need to do everything possible to remove the toxic load. It is here that avoidance of some of the items mentioned could literally save a person's life.

We must be on our guard against all possible maintaining causes, both old and highly-recognised ones, and others that are newcomers to our stage, such as electromagnetic and geopathic stress, and leakage from amalgam fillings in teeth. We must educate people about the ill effects of various things and help turn the tide. First and foremost, we must help people to be responsible for their own health.

The world has changed, people and diseases have changed, as well as our understanding of them. This means that changed methods are now necessary, but we are not at the end of the road. We are just into a new century and "the GM genie is out of the bottle", as Professor Alan Grey, Head of the Centre of Ecology and Hydrology

8 'The Chronic Diseases; Theoretical Part', Samuel Hahnemann, p.183

in Dorset, was quoted as saying in a newspaper article[9]. Few things have had more media attention recently than genetically modified food and genetically modified crops. Little research has been carried out into the long-term affects of these foods, but some studies have found that rats fed on a diet rich in genetically modified corn developed abnormalities in their internal organs and changes to their blood[10]. Scientists have completed The Human Genome Project – deciphering the genetic alphabet of life. We cannot yet say what the effect of genetically modified crops will have on our environment and in turn on our bodies. As we live in a constantly changing world, more may be added on this subject when this book is reprinted.

CHAPTER 4

DIAGNOSTIC WORK

There are various diagnostic techniques for ascertaining the underlying cause of people's problems. Some practitioners rely on electrical devices, such as the Vega machine, or the Synchrometer, a device invented by the physicist Hulda Clark, and some methods are much more 'low tech'. Of course much can be ascertained simply by a thorough consultation, discovering when a problem began and what exacerbates it. Taking the information in this book as a guide, it is essential to find the root of the problem. In order to do this, a practitioner needs to find out what was happening in a patient's life before the problem started, and question them about their lifestyle, work, and nutritional and fluid intake. The writers of this book commonly use a technique known as Diagnostic Kinesiology to aid them in finding the maintaining causes.

9 'The Daily Telegraph', 25th July 2000
10 www.guerillanews.com

Kinesiology is a useful tool based on muscle testing. It is a well-known fact that everything oscillates in a particular frequency or vibration – food, drink, chemicals, metals, parasites, bacteria, etc. The human body also has its own frequency, so if anything causes it harm or benefits it, it resonates accordingly. This is like an opera singer breaking a glass by resonance; the glass is affected by the note she sings, starts to vibrate at the same frequency, and eventually shatters. In her book 'Geopathic Stress', Jane Thurnell-Read states that kinesiology utilises the fact that, when anything stresses the body, it causes muscles to weaken. The American chiropractor Dr. George Goodheart, discovered in 1964 that testing a muscle for strength reveals other things about the body. This led to kinesiology developing beyond an interest in the muscles themselves into using the muscle response as an indicator of other aspects of the body's functioning.

Jóna Ágústa writes:

"I first came across kinesiology on a training course for identifying and treating allergies. Having a healthy amount of scepticism in my nature I felt wary of what seemed a way-out technique, especially when I was told that I had an underactive thyroid. Having no obvious thyroid symptoms just added to my scepticism and I did nothing more to pursue kinesiology. Life has a way of pushing you in directions you resist and when, nine months later, a routine medical test diagnosed an underactive thyroid, I began to take kinesiology a bit more seriously.

I enrolled on an introductory course with The Academy of Systematic Kinesiology and learned a very down-to-earth approach, using kinesiology to find weaknesses in the body and then correcting them. This is a very different approach and relies on material substances for testing, leaving the patient in no doubt as to when an area of her body is weak or when it is strong. It seemed a very thorough and powerful therapy, and once the simple technique of testing was mastered, it was very reliable. I incorporated it in my prac-

tice, initially as a tool for identifying food sensitivities, and later found it a useful tool for the detective work of finding the underlying cause for the disease".

In her book 'Cure for all Diseases', Dr Hulda Clark describes how her work had led her to believe that all disease is caused by a combination of parasites and pollutants. She has had very impressive results in treating all manner of serious conditions, especially cancer; so much so that she had to move her practice across the border to Mexico to avoid US restrictions. She developed a piece of equipment called a synchrometer to identify organisms in the body. Each living organism has its own vibratory frequency and, using the synchrometer, which seems a bit like the early Vega machines, she could identify any abnormal pathogens in the body. She developed a very vigorous method of treatment, which involved ridding the body of parasites and cleansing the body of the toxicity of any pollutants that made a friendly environment for the parasites to thrive in the first place.

The authors had researched into 'maintaining causes' and 'barriers to cure' for the book 'Classical Homœopathy Revisited' and we knew how important it is to try to identify these in order for any health or medical treatment to work truly effectively. We were intrigued by Dr Clark's work – sceptical, but intrigued – so we tried to verify her experiences using kinesiology. We obtained laboratory slides of the main organisms she mentioned and samples of the main pollutants. Then we started testing people using simple Diagnostic Kinesiology (see Appendix 2). We became quite excited when the testing bore out what she had been saying. In particular, we had a lot of success in identifying shigella (a bacteria found in milk) in patients with stubborn sinus problems, generally accompanied by digestive complaints. By using the turmeric and fennel, as suggested by Dr Clark, the symptoms invariably disappeared. We found ascaris in every case of asthma, and strongyloids in every case of migraine. Metals and pollutants were also involved in many cases. We used a herbal parasite programme to rid the body of parasites – very effective, but difficult for children to take (see Appendix 4). In other cases we used her 'Zapper', a resonating electrical device that can kill off parasites in the body.

However, some of Dr Clark's treatment methods are very vigorous and may seem rather extreme, except for the really desperate. In some cases, for instance, she recommends the removal of teeth. Our way of life incorporates so many chemicals and other toxic elements that it is almost impossible to be completely free of them. Using the technique of priority testing – explained a little later – we realised that there were a few baseline maintaining causes that ran through every case, and once these were dealt with, then the parasitic involvement or the food sensitivity, or whatever else had shown up in the original testing, no longer seemed a problem. For example, a little girl who came with 'glue ear' showed sensitivity to dairy products and electromagnetic stress. When we freed her of the electromagnetic stress by using a magnet and demagnetising (see Chapter 7), she was no longer sensitive to dairy products. Her mother then asked if we thought that using a hair dryer on her child nearly every day since birth, as she had been born with extremely thick hair, might have had something to do with her being so sensitive to electricity.

DIAGNOSTIC KINESIOLOGY

The following is a more detailed account of kinesiology and its uses in practice. Kinesiology has been in existence since 1964; firstly developed by chiropractors in America, it is now established as a therapy in its own right. Diagnostic Kinesiology, the name we have given to the way in which we use it, uses the diagnostic capabilities of kinesiology to find where a patient's immune system is failing, to discover the underlying maintaining causes responsible for this failure and to identify any pre-existing barriers to cure. This method can then be used to identify which strengthening factors are most appropriate to remove the maintaining causes and barriers to cure, and to stimulate a healing response in the patient.

Kinesiology is a very effective method of assessing the body's positive and negative energies and can provide a systematic method of analysing a wide range of conditions. When a person is in contact with something that is causing them health problems, their muscles lose tone.

When Samuel Hahnemann wrote '*The Organon*' 200 years ago, he listed many items that he considered to be either a maintaining cause in an illness, or a barrier to the cure of an illness. He thought the body "has to inhibit or exaggerate the excitability or sensitivity of the organism in order to protect itself against complete destruction of life from the hostile attack of such forces" (para. 74). He later stresses the importance of "removing obstacles to cure so that cure is not prevented or impeded". Only after removing barriers to cure and maintaining causes did Hahnemann move on to prescribing homœopathic remedies.

Over the past 50 years there have been steadily worsening conditions for health because of the chemical society that we have now become. There are currently 80,000 man-made chemicals in circulation and over 1,000 are added to this figure every year. The average person has 500 chemicals stored in their fatty tissue, the majority of which did not exist 100 years ago[11].

Dr Hulda Clark has carried out much scientific research into the causes of disease. Her findings have shown her that patients with a variety of different diagnoses have a range of micro-organisms resident in their bodies, in areas where they should not normally be found, or in life cycle stages that are not compatible with

11 Dr Vyvyan Howard, Toxico-pathologist, University of Liverpool

the proper functioning of the human body. She also found that various chemicals – solvents such as benzene, or heavy metals, such as mercury and lead – were present in toxic levels wherever the micro-organisms were present. As an example, all patients presenting with diabetes showed a pancreatic fluke together with methanol (found in processed food) pollution. Dr Clark maintains that the organism likes an environment that is toxic with metals and/or solvents. Now it is well known that there is a strong genetic component here. This means that for some people this increased level of toxicity will lead to, for instance, diabetes, whilst for others it may trigger rheumatism or digestive problems.

Kinesiology has been used since the 1950's to identify food sensitivities and, by using similar techniques and microscopic slides of these organisms, it is possible to verify Dr Clark's results using Diagnostic Kinesiology. By using samples of chemicals, metals and other pollutants it is possible to detect sensitivities to such substances in patients. Using this testing method it is possible to check for problems caused by a range of environmental factors, including solvents, metals, electrical and magnetic fields, pollens, fungi, bacteria, viruses and larger micro-organisms, such as flukes. All of these factors are present in the modern environment and a healthy person lives alongside them without any problems.

Substances such as vaccinations, the contraceptive pill, social drugs, antibiotics and steroids all have known and unknown side effects that cause their own symptoms as the body struggles to cope with its toxicity. Even household chemicals create problems, with washing powders exacerbating, or even causing, skin conditions. Our test kits incorporate all the major brands plus the more environmentally friendly brands (which seem to be tolerated better by those sensitive to washing powders). Once a particular brand is identified as a problem, then it is relatively easy to remove it from the patient's environment.

Kinesiology not only shows up the barriers to cure and maintaining causes, but also the best way to overcome such obstacles, as well as the best-indicated remedies and what strengths to use. In acute illnesses, such as the common cold, influenza and childhood illnesses such as earache, it can show the weakening factors such as a bacteria or virus (often staphylococcus or streptococcus), and it may be found, through kinesiology testing, that the bacteria in a homœopathic potency is the most effective remedy. In chronic illnesses, such as eczema, asthma, migraines or irritable bowel syndrome, kinesiology can reveal a variety of additional weakening factors, such as metals and solvents, simple dehydration, poor nutrition or emotional stress. These can then be addressed in the treatment programme by a variety of measures, including 'tapping' certain acupressure points (see Appendix 2 for more details). Often, once this is done, many symptoms will disappear leaving a clear picture for treatment.

Most cases have just one or two maintaining causes and they will generally be one or more of the following:
- Organisms, such as parasites
- Electrical and/or geopathic stress
- Toxic build-up in the body of substances such as metals and solvents
- Dehydration
- Poor nutrition/food sensitivity
- Emotional stress

Electromagnetic stress is an extremely common maintaining cause. We treat a lot of businesspeople who suffer from it because they are constantly travelling all over the world and are affected by the electromagnetic field of aeroplanes. Their working environments are often large open plan offices with banks of computers. One patient came with constantly itching skin, headaches and general stress symptoms. He was sensitive to several foods and electromagnetic stress and we ascertained that he was commuting to Germany and back each week. Treatment for this is discussed fully in chapter 7, but once this businessman worked on the electromagnetic stress problem, then his symptoms disappeared, as did the food sensitivities.

One of our more recent findings concerns the effects of toxicity from jewellery and body piercings. We had always assumed mercury tooth fillings to be the main culprit when a person showed sensitivity to metals, but were puzzled by several metal-sensitive patients with no amalgam fillings. However, once they removed certain items of jewellery, such as watches or specific body piercings, the weakness vanished.

Dehydration shows up in many cases, especially in those experiencing migraines and chronic headaches. Once this is discovered, the simple expedient of increasing their fluid intake can remove the symptoms in many patients. As has been written, migraine sufferers have the micro-organism strongyloids, but many people carry strongyloids without succumbing to migraines. However, given dehydration and the genetic factor, migraines become a serious problem for some people.

Most people have heard of food sensitivities and are very keen to be checked for these; this fact brings many people into our clinic in the first place. Diagnosing a food sensitivity however is not the cure-all that many patients expect. Whilst removing a certain food from someone's diet may relieve immediate symptoms, it does not get to the root cause of why that person has become allergic in the first place. It often turns out that, if one of the other maintaining causes is removed, then the food is no longer a problem and can easily be tolerated.

Patients often take numerous supplements in the belief that they are beneficial, not realising that they are often wasting their money. Many vitamins are poorly absorbed and can unbalance the system when taken in isolation, but testing can demonstrate which nutritional supplements, if any, are really needed and which are doing no good at all.

Anxieties, phobias and negative emotions, either in the present or left over from some unpleasant occurrence in the past, undermine the immune system. Once identified, a quick and effective technique called Emotional Stress Relief (see Appendix 5), can help alleviate the associated feelings very rapidly, releasing energy to help with the healing process generally. One patient came with many allergies, but was also full of phobias and anxieties ever since an extremely bad experience with LSD many years earlier. The fears it had generated had blighted her life ever since, and she was too scared to even have any homœopathic detoxifying remedies because she had heard that homœopathy might aggravate her symptoms. The Emotional Stress Relief technique was so successful for her that the anxiety and phobias diminished, and she was able to function in the world in a much happier frame of mind.

One of the most useful features provided by Diagnostic Kinesiology is priority testing. Generally we discover more than one sensitivity in each patient, but, by using kinesiology, it is possible to prioritise to find the root sensitivities – usually just one or two factors. Once these are corrected it is often found that the other items or foods, which had been showing up as causing a sensitivity, no longer cause a problem. This can be simply achieved in the consultation and then it is possible to prioritise for the most appropriate medicines, supplements or foods, which will be more effective now that the other weakening factors have been removed.

In terms of patient management this simple non-invasive testing method creates a lot of confidence in, and co-operation from, the patient. He or she can physically experience the weakness caused by a substance that may be contributing to their condition, and this generates a more positive attitude to the treatment being suggested – they will co-operate very willingly with suggested changes to their diet or living habits to assist their recovery. For instance, a teenager came who showed aggressive behaviour after a cola drink, but was refusing to give it up. Once he felt how weak his muscle went when tested with a bottle of the cola drink, he willingly agreed to avoid it, as he played a lot of sport and realised it could affect his performance. This made life easier for the whole family. Conversely, when a patient feels a medicine actually strengthening them, they will have confidence in the treatment they are getting before they even start to take it.

This is how we have developed kinesiology to suit our practice and way of prescribing. It is a flexible tool and practitioners can develop their own way of using it. We always test right from the start so as to quickly identify maintaining causes, straightaway removing a layer, and allowing indicated medicines to work.

DETECTING SENSITIVITIES

One muscle very amenable to this type of testing is pectoralis major clavicular. To utilise this muscle in a kinesiology test, the patient extends their arm straight out in front of them, with elbow locked. In order to see if the muscle is functioning well, the practitioner presses the arm while the patient resists and the arm should hold firm. The practitioner then places a magnet on the pectoralis major clavicular muscle, presses the arm again, and, because the magnet interferes with the electrical functioning of the muscle, the muscle weakens and the arm loses much of its resistance. This process shows the practitioner that the muscle is working as it should. The sample, which can be a bacteria, virus, item of food or drink, or whatever, is then placed on the person's cheek close to the mouth and the arm pressed again. If the arm weakens, the body is 'saying' that this particular sample is harmful. When the practitioner has accurately ascertained the major causative factors, he or she can decide what form of treatment is required to remove them. For a step-by-step approach see Appendix 2.

Although we will discuss the various maintaining causes, the aetiology or triggering factors will vary from patient to patient. Doctors and health practitioners have long been aware of this but were only able to speculate on what we are now able to test with diagnostic techniques such as the one outlined above.

To muscle test babies and infants and those people who are not strong enough to participate in the muscle test themselves, an intermediary person can be used. Just as an electric shock can pass through people, so can their energies. The same procedure is carried out but this time the muscle of an intermediary is tested whilst they have skin to skin contact with the patient. We have found it easy to test a baby for sensitivities using the mother's arm whilst she is breast feeding. Care has to be taken, however, to make sure that the sensitivities found are not those of the intermediary by then testing the intermediary alone with the specific substances.

Once a sensitivity has been detected it may be possible to easily avoid the noxious influence. Alternatively, the patient can be desensitised using a very simple technique which involves tapping a variety of acupressure points – see Appendix 2, Reducing Sensitivities on page 131. We use this technique a lot in our practices. We have been able to desensitise people to a wide range of microbes and environmental substances. For example we have reduced people's susceptibility to hayfever by desensitising them to pollens. Quite often people are allergic to their pets and we ask them to bring in a sample of their pet's fur, so that we can test them with it and desensitise them if required. This technique works by boosting the body's own immune system.

In some cases the patient may not be sensitive but simply overloaded by a substance, e.g. food supplements or metals. In these cases a slightly different acupressure tapping technique is required – see Appendix 2, Limited Tolerance Procedure on page 131.

Both of these acupressure tapping techniques are invaluable in helping to address the maintaining causes. More information can be found by either attending a Diagnostic Kinesiology course at the Newlands Park Clinic or by reading Jane Thurnell-Read's book, *'Health Kinesiology'*.

CHAPTER 5

HORMONES

Hormones travel in bodily fluid and, if we are dehydrated, the body will be less effective at transporting them to where they are most needed. In women at certain times of the month, and at certain stages in life, the body is working hard to eliminate the by-products of hormonal activity. If the kidneys are not able to function at maximum capacity, then the skin, the largest eliminative organ of the body, must take over and symptoms such as hot sweats may result. Also, if the body is eradicating toxic hormonal by-products monthly and there are other toxins already in the system, then during menstruation the body can get overwhelmed and unable to eliminate efficiently; P.M.T., spots and other symptoms can then result.

Therefore the main factors which we are addressing in the book are relevant to the hormonal cycle. Emotional stresses can also affect the secretion of the ovaries in different ways, and a disturbance of these glands can cause period pain, premenstrual tension and even a complete cessation of menses.

However, there are other factors to consider when discussing hormones; one of them is 'The Pill', which is taken worldwide by around 100 million women. The Pill works by preventing ovulation, suppressing the body's natural function. There has been much research into its side effects and there is evidence linking it to breast cancer, strokes, heart attacks and blood clots. However, as well as affecting the individual, the pill has far-reaching consequences socially. In the U.K. we have to tolerate recycled tap water that includes oestrogen from the urine of pill users along with oestrogen-mimicking chemical phthalates (by-products of plastic breakdown). The latter also gets into our food and the U.K. Ministry of Agriculture has invariably found phthalates in samples of meat, fish, eggs, milk and milk products taken since 1993.

> *"While studying lake water for pesticide contamination, chemists at a Swiss agricultural research laboratory found an unexpected pollutant: clofibric acid, a drug for lowering cholesterol. Once they started looking, European researchers found lipid-lowering drugs, analgesics (including ibuprofen and diclofenac), beta-blocker heart drugs, chemotherapy drugs, antibiotics, and hormones in water bodies that supply drinking water. Higher concentrations were found in more populated areas. Having ruled out industrial spillage, researchers realised that the drugs had come from human body wastes."*[12]

How much of a drug gets broken down by the body varies depending on the drug and on the individual. Between 50% and 90% of a medicine, in its original form, may be excreted from the body. Sometimes, chemical reactions with the environment turn partly degraded drugs back into an active form[13].

On 17th March 2002, the BBC's 'Country File' programme revealed the contents of a leaked report stating

12 This appeared in 'Wildlife News', 18th December 1999, taken from 'Pharmaceutical Residues in Europe's Water' (Nexus, Vol 6, no. 5):

13 'Drugged Waters' by Janet Raloff, published in Townsend Letter for Doctors & Patients, no. 192, July 1999.

that the artificial female hormone used in the human contraceptive pill – as well as natural female hormones – could be responsible for reducing the fertility of male fish. The programme also implied that there could be a further connection with declining human male fertility.

All this means that we are constantly being bombarded with synthetic oestrogen and this can affect people in one of two ways. It can mean that the balance of the body is affected because receiving so much oestrogen leaves it unable to produce oestrogen effectively by itself. This works in just the same way as when the body is given artificial steroids, or thyroxin or insulin, in sufficient quantity that it results in the atrophy of the adrenal glands, thyroid gland or pancreas; the body is less able to produce the hormones and secretions by itself. Alternatively, we can have a situation where, because of excess oestrogen upsetting the body's balance, we are unable to produce sufficient progesterone to compensate.

It is in these circumstances that herbal medicines are very useful. Where used properly herbal medicines can work to normalise, regulate and balance the body's natural functions. They can provide raw materials, and, in ways not completely understood, they can teach the body what it needs to be doing by itself. This cannot happen when active ingredients are synthesised. When chemical drugs are used they work like the synthetic oestrogen previously described; as the body is receiving plenty of artificial hormones it often becomes lazy in its own work of producing and balancing hormones, so that eventually it just comes to rely totally on the drugs.

Herbal remedies do not need to be taken indefinitely. Usually two to three months is long enough for them to 'teach' the body what it needs to produce to make up any shortfall.

WILD YAM

There are three herbal remedies that we commonly use for menstrual and menopausal symptoms. The first option is Wild Yam (*Dioscorea villosa*), which was, at one time, the sole source of the chemicals used as the raw materials for the manufacture of the contraceptive pill. It is used in the laboratory to make progesterone and other hormones, but it does not, of itself, contain progesterone. Exaggerated claims have been made about it being a substitute for progesterone, but whilst there is scope for more research, it does appear to help the body make much better use of the hormone, and can be little short of a 'miracle cure', when it is indicated. The people who fare best with this herb are those for whom a homœopath might prescribe Sepia[14].

Now, not all of these symptoms need to be present, but if they do cover a woman's main hormonal reactions, then Dioscorea will often be of great benefit. It should not be used during pregnancy, but otherwise we have never encountered any side effects, although some literature states that it can cause nausea and diarrhoea if used in extremely large amounts. The usual dosage would be 5-10 drops of the diluted tincture three times daily, but this could be doubled at times of the menstrual cycle, depending on symptoms e.g. before the menses in women with PMT.

Not to be be taken during pregnancy.

14 This means that it is particularly helpful for women who, at time of menses, ovulation or menopause, suffer from a lack of energy, depression, irritability or sensitivity so that they are easily offended, and misconstrue what is said to them. There can be an aversion to company and they do not want the sympathy of friends or family (although they have a dread of being alone also). They become sulky, indifferent and irritable under pressure. They may complain about their memory and take on many worries that would not normally affect them.

BLACK COHOSH

The second herb that we commonly use is Black Cohosh or *Cimicifuga racemosa,* an important herb which has come to us from the Native Americans. It is a 'normaliser' and relaxant of the female reproductive system, and can often be used beneficially in delayed and painful menstruation. It has a normalising action on the balance of female sex hormones, particularly the oestrogen levels, and may be safely used to regain normal hormonal activity. This again can help with hot flushes and premenstrual tension. It is one of the most useful remedies to use during the menopause for such symptoms as hot flushes and vaginal dryness. The symptoms that would suggest a prescription of Black Cohosh are those for which a homœopath would often suggest the remedy Pulsatilla[15], which works more on the oestrogen axis.

Again the herb should be avoided if pregnant or breast-feeding and it may interfere with hormonal medications, such as the contraceptive pill. People taking medication for hypertension should also use it with caution, as it could intensify the drug's effect of lowering blood pressure. Apart from this, the herb has no known side effects, although in some people very large quantities have been reported as causing stomach upsets, nausea and headaches. In our many years of clinical experience, however, we have never found these side effects when using the tincture at a dosage of 5 or 10 drops diluted in a little water, three times daily.

Not to be be taken during pregnancy.

15 Such a woman would be changeable in mood, but also mild, timid, tearful, discouraged, easily offended and touchy; the overriding factor, however, is the need for emotional support. They can find decision-making very difficult and can lean heavily on other people, needing reassurance, consolation and all the embraces offered to them!

AGNUS CASTUS

The third herb is *Agnus Castus* or Chaste Berry, which stimulates the pituitary gland into producing the correct levels of progesterone, oestrogen, testosterone and many other hormones necessary for normal body functioning. It has become well-known as a hormonal regulator for women and is extremely helpful in alleviating a wide range of pre-menstrual problems such as spots, irritability, breast tenderness, premenstrual migraine and bloating. It can help to regulate a woman's menstrual cycle, improve fertility, lengthen out a short cycle and even restore menstruation in a woman who has stopped her periods (although the underlying cause of this should always be investigated), and it can restore the body's hormonal balance after using the contraceptive pill or H.R.T. For women entering the menopause, it can help to even out mood swings and relieve hot flushes. Men can use *Agnus Castus* too, for acne. It should however be avoided in conditions associated with relative progesterone excess and it should not be used if taking any form of hormonal medication, such as H.R.T. or the pill. Often it will help with menstrual or menopausal problems in cases where Lachesis[16] could be the appropriate homœopathic remedy.

Not to be be taken during pregnancy.

16 The general symptom complex here is of women with an assertive temperament, liable to temper outbursts, loquacity and jealousy at certain times of the menstrual cycle. Many symptoms are relieved by the onset of menses and being in the open air, whilst the constriction of tight clothing may exacerbate them.

It is never necessary for a person to exhibit all the given symptoms for the medicine to work, but rather that the medicine is suitable to treat their main symptoms. As a general guide, if a herbal tincture has been taken for a three-month period then it is good to have a break for a month before starting again if necessary. This generally prevents any side effects, or 'provings', as they are sometimes called. If anything that is not in a complete food balance is taken for an excessive amount of time, it can produce effects which may be the opposite of those desired. For instance, hops are often consumed or added to pillows to aid sleep. People who used to go hop-picking in Kent every summer slept very well at the beginning of the season, but by the end many were suffering from insomnia because they had inhaled too much of the volatile oils. In the same way, taking any herbal or homœopathic medicine to excess may produce, for a short time, the symptoms that they were designed to cure. The standard dose used for herbal tinctures is 5-10 drops, three times daily, which may be doubled at certain times of the menstrual cycle if symptoms are more pronounced.

CHAPTER 6

WATER

It is very fashionable to proceed with food exclusion diets and to give patients a long list of foods that are to be avoided. Yet Nature made us able to consume a variety of foods and, if someone has a problem with many foods, then normally we need to find the underlying factor. Deal with this factor and, more often than not, the foods will no longer cause a problem.

One of these factors is dehydration, of which there are three main causes: (a) not drinking enough water, (b) consuming that which dehydrates and (c) an organism that takes fluid and nutrition at the host's expense.

We all have a 'bank account' of fluid, which is taken into credit by drinking water. This includes the water content of drinks such as herb teas, barley, chicory or similar grain drinks, squashes and fruit juices. Few people, however, drink enough. Despite increasing sales of bottled water, actual consumption is small in relation to need because many people simply carry them as a fashion accessory, taking only occasional sips.

On the other hand, this 'bank account' is debited by heat, humidity, exercise, caffeine, alcohol, and salt. Even carbonated water is of limited benefit; carbon dioxide gives carbonated drinks their fizz, but the body has to eliminate it.

Among the patients attending our clinics it is very common to find stressed business people who suffer badly with headaches. Many of them start the day with a cup of tea, then drink coffee continually while at work and then use alcohol to help them unwind in the evening. This results in a permanent state of dehydration, with symptoms that may be similar to a hangover, as both alcohol and caffeine can 'dry out' the brain. Many of these people spend their lives taking pain killers, when, in effect, less caffeine and a few glasses of water each day would eliminate not only the symptoms, but also the true cause of the problem.

A woman, 60 years old, came with a chronic bladder infection. She had had many courses of antibiotics, which did not relieve the problem. She was in a wheelchair as a result of MS and was very embarrassed about going to the toilet because her husband had to carry her. Therefore she did not drink any water and only had two cups of coffee and tea during the morning. After increasing her water consumption, her bladder infection disappeared. Dehydration was her maintaining cause.

A 55-year-old man had had an irritating cough for five years. He had undergone all kinds of tests and had been treated with various drugs. These only palliated, and the situation got worse. For 20 years he had worked in the building industry, and was regularly covered with dust. His daily intake of coffee and tea was 4-6 cups, and no water. His cough improved rapidly as soon as he increased his water consumption.

A schoolgirl, 17 years old, with a diagnosed irritable bladder, drank very little to try to avoid leaving the classroom every lesson to relieve herself. After being told by the practitioner to increase her fluid intake, the problem disappeared in three weeks. In fact, schools used to be one of the worst places for encouraging dehydration, both for teachers, who had just tea and coffee at break time, and for the children, who were not allowed to drink in the classroom. A water fountain in the cold playground or in the toilets (with dubious hygiene) were the only possibilities for obtaining a drink. We used to have to write letters to the school asking for our children to be allowed to drink during lessons. Fortunately the situation is changing as educationalists are waking up to the fact that increased water consumption helps with memory, concentration and academic skills, because the brain is nourished by water-carrying oxygen. Proper hydration may also help to reduce mental confusion in the elderly, who often drink only tea or coffee. In care homes for the elderly the tea and coffee trolley regularly appears, but there is little or no encouragement to drink water.

Interestingly, dehydration is more common in the winter months than during the summer. In the summer we feel the sun upon us and we are aware of perspiring; we feel thirsty and we drink, more often cold drinks, such as water and fruit juice. During the winter months we are often in the hot, centrally heated environment of our home, school or office, and we dehydrate slowly, gradually, without realising it. We are not aware of our perspiration because it dries immediately. We drink more hot drinks in the cold weather for comfort, and these tend to be the caffeine-based drinks tea and coffee. It is worth noting that if you ask for a cappuccino when on holiday somewhere such as Greece, a glass of water is often provided with it. In Iceland, a great coffee-drinking nation, a coffee house will usually provide a jug of water and glasses for patrons to help themselves. In England, however, it is sometimes difficult or impossible to obtain water in a restaurant or café without being asked to pay a significant amount for a bottle.

A rather odd comment sometimes heard from dehydrated patients is, "I do not like drinking water as it makes me thirsty!" The logic here is that if we have been dehydrated for a long time then our body's reflexes shut down and no longer tell us of the fact. In the same way, if we live in a land of famine and drought, then we begin not to feel thirsty. Food parcels then arrive, we eat or drink and our bodies wake up to tell us what we need, bringing back the desire for food or water.

Where our body's natural instincts have not been dulled by years of incorrect feeding, listening more closely to their natural desires can, of itself, bring an improvement in health. It should however be said that this is more reliable in acute disease where the desire for certain drinks, foods and rest is quite marked. Too often in chronic disease the body's desires and cravings have been eroded away by a habit of fast and convenience foods.

PARASITES

Another cause of dehydration is parasites, which take fluid and nutrition at the expense of a human host. Although many people may associate the word 'parasite' with diseases in Africa or Asia, having parasites is much more common in modern Western society than might be imagined. One of the most common parasites is taenia.

A parasite is any organism that lives in or on another organism, at the expense of that other organism. A host is any animal that harbours a parasite. "There is no part of man's body, nor, indeed, any part of the bodies of hosts of parasitic animals in general, which is not visited by some kind of parasitic animal at some time or other during their life histories"[17]. This means that parasites, including fungi, can occur anywhere in our body, in any organ. Our blood, muscles, heart, lungs, and brain are all possible sites for parasitic infestation.

The research of Dr Hulda Clark led her to write,

> *"Our bodies harbor numerous stages of tapeworms (taenia). But not the tapeworm itself, which may belong to a dog, cow or pigeon. Tapeworms lead complicated lives, much like insects with their caterpillars, larvae, larval molts, pupae and eventual adults ...... Whatever animal species you live near, or once lived near, you probably swallowed some of its filth and some tape eggs. The eggs hatch in your stomach and the tiny larvae burrow into a neighbouring organ without any consideration that this is your stomach wall or spleen or muscle"* *(The Cure for all Diseases).*

17 Lapage, G. Animals Parasitic in Man. Dover Publications 1957

As we eat with unwashed hands or after touching animals, so we swallow quantities of tapeworm eggs, ascaris and other organisms. If susceptible, a diet rich in pumpkin seeds, cider vinegar, jasmine tea and carrot juice will help eliminate taenia and other parasites from the gut. Acupressure 'tapping' as described in Appendix 2 can immediately render us less sensitive.

Sometimes we see patients who are dehydrated complaining of headaches. Despite their pain initially reducing after a drink of water, it can return after a brief interlude. Sometimes water can make an immediate difference, but not always if a parasite or fungus is leaching water from the body.

We are reminded of a patient with constipation, a dry mouth and a considerable thirst. As constipation can be aggravated by dehydration it was suggested that she drink more water, at which point she burst into tears saying that it would be impossible for her to drink any more. This then led us to look for a parasite. Finding taenia, she was put on a diet including ample pumpkin seeds, and the condition improved rapidly. Under these conditions parasites and fungi are normally involved and can be dealt with by de-sensitising the patient using acupressure (see Appendix 2).

For long-term benefit when dealing with parasites, herbal remedies such as pumpkin seeds, carrot juice, cider vinegar, green tea and CoQ10 are more effective. The seeds of the pumpkin have long been used for the apparently mechanical act of expelling worms and tapeworm, or a parasite cleanse programme can be carried out (see Appendix 4).

We would emphasise, however, that very rarely do we treat a patient with a tapeworm. Very frequently though we do find tapeworm stages in a person, which, in another animal, might lead to a tapeworm, but in a human may not even be found in a conventional stool test. This may be due either to their microscopic nature or because the taenia easily burrow through the cell membranes of the gut to the weaker and more vulnerable organs. If an organ is in a more toxic or septic state due, for example, to poor diet, smoking or drugs, it is here that any pathogenic parasite or micro-organism will wish to set up home. It will then add to the toxicity by its own waste products and problems then begin or worsen.

As an effective treatment for taenia we regularly prescribe capsules containing organic pumpkin seeds, with a small amount of garlic, cayenne, thyme and cramp bark (Scallywag, available from www.traditionalhealth.co.uk). The latter ingredient helps symptoms, whilst the former are powerful herbal antiseptics or vermifuges. As the taenia could probably tolerate the effect of a single capsule daily, we usually recommend a dose of 3-6 capsules each day. Snacking on pumpkin seeds is also helpful and they can be easily obtained from local health food shops or supermarkets. In most cases this treatment causes the taenia problem to disappear after about three weeks, although, if the condition has been long-standing, it may take longer as a greater quantity of the pumpkin seeds, capsules and or oil will need to be consumed.

An additional product to supplement and augment this treatment is co-enzyme Q10. CoQ10 is essential for all energy production in our cells. Studies show that most people over 35 have CoQ10 deficiency, and that obese people may be up to 50% deficient. It is taken daily by over 6 million Japanese and by 20% of the adults in health-conscious Denmark. The benefits of taking CoQ10 include: increased energy, improved athletic performance, help with weight loss and improved gum condition.

According to Hulda Clark[18] it takes a large amount, 3-4 gms, of CoQ10 to eliminate taenia in some places, such as the brain or bone marrow. As CoQ10 is found in every cell and is never toxic, there are no side effects, but cost may prohibit large quantities being used on a regular

18 'The Cure for HIV and Aids', p.35

basis. If, however, the treatment with pumpkin seeds is insufficient, CoQ10 should be added, as well as the use of methods described in Appendix 2.

A 40-year-old woman with alternating constipation and diarrhoea was diagnosed with irritable bowel syndrome. She was dehydrated, and a glass of water made an immediate difference to cramping in the bowel. However, after about 50 minutes the cramps returned. Taenia was suspected, and a diet rich in pumpkin seeds and carrot juice relieved all of her symptoms until she stopped this regimen and all her problems returned. She then added pumpkin seed capsules (Scallywag), CoQ10 and cider vinegar to her routine and all symptoms disappeared over the next few weeks. She now keeps her colon healthy by just adding pumpkin seeds to her muesli or salad.

Interestingly, taenia is very rarely found in Iceland or England over the winter months. Perhaps it survives on the fur of animals or on fruit and vegetables during the summer, but is killed off during the colder weather. More research could be done, as at the moment we can only speculate.

WHICH WATER TO DRINK?

It is recommended that we drink at least 8 glasses of water a day, the key words being "at least". However, we are faced with many different sources of water: filtered, tap, bottled. Which of these are most beneficial for our health?

BOTTLED WATER

Sales in bottled water have increased dramatically over the last decade, making it a $4 billion-a-year business in the United States. Supermarkets now have whole aisles dedicated to varieties of bottled water: mineral, spring and table. However, the findings of the Natural Resources

Defense Council (NRDC) found that although "most bottled water apparently is of good quality, some contain contamination; it should not be automatically assumed to be purer or safer than most tap water" (www.nrdc.org). Both spring and table water have been treated chemically before bottling. After bottling it can take a long time for the water to be sold, meaning that the water isn't 'fresh'. This storage time exacerbates the hazards of drinking bottled water as bacteria have time to colonise; "staphylococcus and E.Coli are commonly seen" says Hulda Clark.
Also, bottled water can contain phthalates, a group of chemicals used in most modern plastics to make them more pliable. These phthalates 'leak' from the plastic bottles into the water; longer storage time means more phthalates in the water[19]. Phthalates levels are regulated in tap water by EPA (Environmental Protection Agency), but the FDA (Food and Drug Administration) does not regulate it in bottled water. The health issues associated with phthalates is that they have been shown to mimic oestrogen and have been linked to fertility problems[20]. To avoid this contamination the storage of water in glass bottles is preferable, but this is not always practical.

As more and more research is being carried out into bottled water, the findings are quite shocking. Professor Shotyk from Heidelberg University, Germany, has found alarmingly high levels of antimony in bottled water. The water absorbs this element from the plastic by the process of leaching. Antimony is poisonous and even in small amounts can cause headaches, dizziness and depression.[21]

TAPWATER

Tap water is cheap and readily accessible; also as it is from a flowing water source it does not have time to become stagnant and contaminated with bacteria.

19 www.nrdc.org/water/drinking/bw/chep1.asp
20 Jane Thurnell-Read, www.btconnect.co.uk/lifework/lifeworknews
21 Metro, 13th March 2006

However, due to extensive recycling, English water does contain a lot of chemicals – including chlorine, fluorine, drugs and hormones.

The amount of fluoride varies according to where you live, as some water authorities deliberately 'fluoridate' the water. Fluoridation schemes were first introduced in the United States in 1946. Since the 1960s about 10% of the UK receives fluoridated water supplies and decreases in dental decay in those areas were attributed to this. The government wants to extend fluoridation of water to more areas. This is a controversial issue as anti-fluoridation campaigners claim increased fluorine is linked to cancer, osteoporosis, low IQ in children and abnormalities such as Down's Syndrome[22].

According to the British Fluoridation Society, one of the ways in which fluoride works is by "inhibiting the function of enzymes" which cause the build-up of acids which leads to tooth decay[23]. However, the chances that just these enzymes are affected and not others seems small. There is concern that fluorine is an 'enzyme poison' and Dr. Richard Capps from Chicago found evidence that fluorine displaces iodine in the body and in turn disrupts thyroid function[24].

Therefore drinking tap water can pose some health issues, especially in areas where fluoridation occurs. Some people just don't like the taste of it, and there may be a valid reason for this. For further reading, '*The Fluoride Deception*' by Christopher Bryson covers a lot of history and research into this issue. Hulda Clark says,

> *"Your own tap water is not pure (indeed it may have up to 500 toxic elements)".*

Trace amounts of solvents can also be found in bottled water as they are used in the bottling process, and these are not beneficial. Also, researchers claim that the urine from women taking the birth control pill is causing hor-

22 www.society.guardian.co.uk/publichealth/story/0,,994177,00.html
23 www.guardian.co.uk/analysis.story/0,,984313,00.html
24 www.guardian.co.uk/g2/story/0,,1233560,00html

monally active chemicals to be present in our water supplies and may be causing a decline in sperm counts. It is known that chemicals that act like oestrogen can have dramatic effects on animals, for example turning some fish into hermaphrodites[25].

FILTERED WATER

Hulda Clark says that water filters are not the answer as they simply trap the contaminants and then just leak them out into any water that is filtered through the same filter. However she does say that a carbon filter replaced every month may improve your tap water.

In our research we have found that the carbon water filters which are readily available in shops produce water which is actually harmful to the body. Upon muscle testing (see Appendix 2) we found that samples of this type of filtered water actually weakened the muscle. Upon further investigation we found that this water appears to affect the mineral composition of the body and patients drinking this water suffered from mineral and vitamin deficiencies. We now recommend that people do not use these carbon filters.

One type of filter that does not appear to be detrimental and produces water that not only tastes nice and is beneficial to the body is the 'Wellness' water filter, which originates from Japan and consist of a 3 phase system:

1) purification,
2) energetic activation,
3) enhancement.

It increases the oxygen content and negative ions present in the water.

IN CONCLUSION

There are pros and cons for each source of water available to us, but whatever the source it is important that

25 New Scientist' 18th April 2001

we drink enough to maintain our health. Ideally, more research and investment is needed to improve the quality of tap water so that everyone benefits.

CHAPTER 7

ELECTROMAGNETIC STRESS

Few things are as interwoven in our modern life as electricity. But electricity, like so many other things that we have mastered for our progress and convenience, has shown itself to be a double-edged sword. While being our friend, providing light and warmth, it can also be dangerous to our health. Our use of electrical energy for power and communication has led to electrical pollution, which not only threatens ourselves as individuals, but also our common home – the planet Earth.

The Earth has its own natural electromagnetic field, which results mainly from the interaction between its magnetic field and the energy from the sun. The Earth's magnetic field is produced by electric currents which the rotation of the Earth creates in the molten metals found within its core. For millions of years we have lived in harmony with this background electromagnetism and under the protection of the Earth's atmosphere, but through our progress we have created artificial electromagnetic radiation, which is very different from these natural fields, and has changed the balance of the total electromagnetic field of the Earth.

ELECTRICAL BOMBARDMENT

The growth of electric power and communication systems has been non-stop in the last 50 years and new technologies are appearing and progressing every day. They are everywhere in our industrial world and also outside it, where our satellites bombard the Earth with microwaves.

We do not, however, have to go as far out as space to get a glimpse of the picture; a quick glance around our home is enough. We see the lights, the heaters, radios, refrigerators, microwave ovens, stoves, computers, vacuum cleaners, telephones and televisions, to name but a few items. Every power line and electrical appliance produces an electromagnetic field that radiates out from it and all these household appliances radiate electric waves, which bombard the human body and can result in abnormalities in its physiology and function.

The change from a natural environment to our electro-technical world was slow, but now the changes occur every day – almost every minute. The 3G generation of mobile phones with wireless Internet is now with us, the latest step in changing the total electromagnetic field of the Earth.

Living in this new world has a profound effect on people's health. The effect of 'electromagnetic stress' is a fairly new phenomenon; the first cases and discussions came to public knowledge in the early 1970s and today it is recognised as a common illness and a frequent maintaining cause.

A health report in the magazine 'Zest' began,

"Mobiles, microwaves, hairdryers. Every day, you're woken up by a clock radio – before switching on the light, boiling the kettle, opening the fridge and catching a bit of breakfast TV. Before you leave the house, you chuck your mobile in your bag and dash to work to start tapping away at your computer, under fluorescent lights. Your whole life revolves around electricity, so the last thing you want to hear is that it could be doing you harm. But according to consumer pressure group Powerwatch, all of the above could be implicated in the increasing incidence of electromagnetic stress (EMS)."

This is backed up by a Swedish survey which found that possibly 3 percent of the population suffer from extreme adverse reactions to electromagnetic fields (EMFs)[26].

A headline in 'The Daily Mirror', 10th Jan 2002, read "Hairdryers double the chance of miscarriage", and the subsequent article added that vacuum cleaners and travelling regularly on electric trains or trams could have the same effect. It quoted the research of a US scientist, Mr Do-Kun Li of Oakland, California, who studied more than 1000 women in their first ten weeks of pregnancy. He said that electromagnetic fields below the recommended safe levels of 1600 microteslas were high enough to disrupt cell communication, leading to possible miscarriage. He concluded that if women were regularly in contact with such fields, then the risk was trebled.

Around the same time 'The Daily Mail' carried a headline, "Leukaemia risk from hairdryers". It mentioned potential problems from hairdryers, shavers, can openers and household wiring, whilst saying that washing machines with powerful motors are shielded by metal and are less likely to be a problem. The international research that examined the dangers of electric pylons also discovered a link between electromagnetic fields and Motor Neurone Disease. In the UK an Oxford University team studied 35,000 medical records and concluded that children living within 100 metres of overhead power lines had almost twice the risk of developing leukaemia[27].

As it is not easy to draw watertight conclusions, the scientific world is divided as to the validity of some of this research. A US scientist said, "There's a risk in these things getting over-interpreted and scaring the dickens out of people". However in all branches of the scientific community many experts are concerned, and in our clinics we find that electromagnetic stress is one of the main contributing factors to the ill health of our patients.

26 Johansson, O. 'What Doctors Don't Tell You', April 2005, Vol 16 no1
27 unpublished report by Draper G et al. in 'The Times', 30th October 2004

Jane, a 28-year-old solicitor from London, began to feel unwell after she had moved house. She was using her bedroom as an office, and it therefore contained her computer and answering machine. She began feeling permanently exhausted and irritable, but reported that her health and energy returned once these two items were removed from the room. Indeed, chronic fatigue is regularly associated with electromagnetic stress, as are many conditions that affect the electric systems in the body, including multiple sclerosis, epilepsy and Parkinson's disease.

Despite all the research into finding a cure for cancer, the incidence of the disease is rising, and it has not escaped people's notice that, as the rate of cancer has increased, so has the use of computers, mobile phones and the radio masts and other equipment that support them. So can there be a link between the two? Why would we be so affected by electromagnetism? Robert Becker, amongst others including the French biologist Jacques Benveniste, showed that the human body has its own very low-level natural EMFs. These fields are used in the body in many health-healing processes, and can help explain how homœopathy works. They showed that the cells in the body communicate through subtle electromagnetic and quantum frequencies. This again gives further evidence that fundamentally we are electromagnetic beings, and therefore affected by other electromagnetic fields.

Emma, a 30 year old from Glasgow, was suffering from bad headaches. She reported that these ceased when she moved to an office without a large number of fluorescent lights. Jean Philips, spokesperson for Powerwatch, explained, *"We're all made up of cells, which communicate in two different ways – chemically and electrically. Research shows that electromagnetic fields can prevent, or distort, communication between cells. As the brain cells are more active than the physical cells that make up our bodies, we often notice the cognitive effects of electromagnetic fields (headaches, forgetfulness) first."*

The US National Council on Radiation Protection claims that certain household appliances, like food mixers and vacuum cleaners, produce enough electricity to promote Parkinson's disease, Alzheimer's disease, cancer and coronary heart disease. It recommends safety levels 8000 times lower than the current British danger level.

Currently in the UK, acceptable EMF levels are 100μT (microteslas). In Sweden it is 0.2μT, 500 times lower than the UK! "Medical evidence shows that the number of childhood leukaemia cases roughly doubles at 0.2μT, and triples at over 0.35μT, levels way below the UK official guidelines"[28].

EMFs drop dramatically the further you are from the source. The table below shows the EMFs of common household appliance[29].

Appliance	Up Close (μT)	One Metre Away (μT)
Electric razor	2000	0.3
Hairdryer	2000	0.3
Vacuum cleaner	800	2.0
Television set	50	0.2
Washing Machine	50	0.2
Bedside Clock	50	0.02
Fridge	2	0.02
Electric Blanket	3	–

It is also interesting to note that when travelling on electric trains, the EMFs in the carriages are at an average of 1.6μT, with higher levels found at the ends of the carriages.

It can be seen looking at this table that most of the appliances are way above the UK recommended safety limits, let alone Swedish ones. This table links into what

28 Annu Rev Public Health,2004;e-pub
29 What Doctors Don't Tell You', April 2005, Vol 16 no1

we are witnessing in our clinics. Some patients are so sensitive that they are weakened from the EMFs produced by their watches! All go weak when a hairdryer is directed at them, yet this appliance is used daily by a large proportion of the population!

Icelandic electrical technician, Valdimar Valdimarsson, talks in one of his lectures about three kinds of electrical pollution; electric field, electromagnetic field and radio waves. Valdimarsson recollects how discussions about electromagnetic stress started in Sweden. Doctors dealt with case after case of people suffering from intolerance to electrical devices – often people who had worked for years with computers or other electrical tools. The most common symptoms at an early stage were stinging in the face (as from sunburn), itching, and persistent headache and, in later stages, joint pains, dizziness, nausea, photophobia, hypersensitivity to smell and sound and chronic fatigue. When research into these symptoms began, sceptics called them 'The Swedish Syndrome'. That name received quite another meaning when Olle Johansen at the Karolinska Institutet in Sweden led a study that showed, without doubt, the existence of electromagnetic stress (ES)[30].

In 1998, a survey was carried out by a Swedish trade union on ES symptoms[31]. They found the organs most affected were the eyes and skin. Other symptoms were headaches, fatigue, loss of concentration and short-term memory, depression, breathlessness, excessive thirst, numbness, weakness and painful joints.

In the USA, Dr William Rae came to the same conclusion in his own personal case, as Dr Robert O. Becker tells in his book 'Cross Currents'. A former surgeon from Texas, Dr Rae found that his allergic and neurological symptoms were caused by the electromagnetic fields in

30 Morgunbla□i□(Valdimarsson, Valdimar: Lecture in the Nordic House 29.4'97)

31 Swedish Union of Clerical and Technical Employees. Hypersensitivity in IT Environments. Stockholm 1998

the operating room. He then established his own clinic, the Environmental Health Center, in Dallas, Texas, where, through highly scientific research, he proved that electromagnetic stress is a real disease[32].

Since this research was carried out there has been a growing interest in electromagnetic stress and a great deal more research is being undertaken. In 'Cross Currents' there are many examples of studies into the health hazards of being exposed to man-made electrical fields. Becker states that all abnormal, man-made electromagnetic fields, regardless of their frequencies, produce the same biological effects, which deviate from normal functions and are actually, or potentially, harmful.

Both Becker and Valdimarsson cite research and many cases, and discuss the connection between electromagnetic fields and chronic fatigue, Alzheimer's disease, Parkinson's disease, cancer and mental diseases, to name just a few. For example, Valdimarsson quotes research done by Professor Per-Arne Öckerman, head physician at the University Clinic in Lund, Sweden, along with Professor Christer Tageson. They discovered a method to measure the damage caused by electromagnetic fields by analysing the patient's urine and excrement. They state that the cells of patients suffering from electromagnetic stress are clearly damaged – both the membrane and the DNA core. This is supported by research done by American scientists at the University of Washington, in Seattle, who have reported finding "magnetic-field-induced DNA strand breaks" in the cells of laboratory rats subjected to EMFs [33].

Over a decade ago researchers at the Swedish National Institute of Occupational Health concluded a 19-year-long study into the increased risk of various diseases among electrical workers, and a clear pattern emerged. Consistently, these workers were found to have an

32 Becker, R,O. Cross Currents. The Startling Effects of Electromagnetic Radiation on Your Health. Bloomsbury Publications,(UK) 1996

33 Environ Health Perspect, 2004; 112:687-94

increased risk of two types of cancer – brain tumours and leukaemia. There was a relatively consistent dose-response, too: by and large, the greater the EMF exposure, the higher the risk of cancer[34].

This is also consistent with what we are finding in our clinics. One of the common factors that patients with cancer are suffering from is electromagnetic stress (see Chapter 10).

MOBILE PHONES

One of the discussions about dangers from electrical devices is on the use of mobile phones and the problems caused by their emission of microwave radiation. Some research has been carried out on the dangers of using mobile phones without some form of protection.

As we write in 2009, a decade-long investigation overseen by the World Health Organisation (WHO) known as the "Interphone Enquiry" is poised to publish evidence of a "significantly increased risk" of some brain tumours "related to use of mobile phones for a period of 10 years or more." However, the publishing of the final report has been delayed for years as industry co-sponsors are alleged to be arguing over how to present the results.

A report for the British government by Sir William Stewart of Tayside University stated that using mobile phones could cause "biological effects – even though there is no evidence of any risk – and that care should be taken in their use, particularly by children, and that calls using such phones should be kept as short as possible".

We are asked to turn off our mobile phones in aeroplanes because their microwaves can, possibly, affect the controls; but we are still debating if, and how, to protect ourselves, thus gambling on how much our bodies can tolerate before our own controls are adversely affected. Aeroplanes are specially protected from the bombardment of rays from space. "Shields or screens have been

34 British Journal of Industrial Medicine.1991;48:597-603

used to protect highly sensitive equipment against very strong cosmic rays (weather, satellites, etc.)"[35]. But the pilots, the human beings flying the planes, are not specifically protected. Icelandic research has shown that Icelandic pilots are in tenfold danger of getting skin cancer compared to their non-pilot peers. This research was carried out by Professor Vilhjálmur Rafnsson at the University of Iceland's medical faculty, Jón Hrafnkelsson, specialist in cancer therapy and Hrafn Tulinius, chief physician of the Icelandic Cancer Society. Their findings were published in the British magazine 'Occupational and Environmental Medicine' (Jónsson,Á.Morgunbla□i□. 19th November 1995). We see patients who are pilots or stewardesses often complaining of tiredness and suffering from electromagnetic stress, because they spend much of their time in a big metal electronic box in the sky.

Tsuyoshi Hondou, a researcher from Tohoku University in Japan, concluded that "Passengers on packed trains could unwittingly be exposed to electromagnetic fields far higher than those recommended under international guidelines. The problem? Hordes of commuters all using their mobile phones at the same time." This could well be a major environmental problem, especially as new wireless devices and laptop "connections" come onto the market. He suggests that train operators should take notice. Presently there are no regulations as to the use of mobile phones in areas where a lot of people may be gathered.

Some mobile phone companies have had cases brought against them in court by people who claim to have developed tumours as a result of exposure to their products. Dr Lennart Hardell, a Swedish cancer specialist, found that mice exposed to the radiation emitted by mobile phones were 2.5 times more likely to develop brain tumours. Cordless phones emit electromagnetic fields and can have a similar effect. Opinion is divided about the use of

35 Schimmel, H.W. Guidelines for the Treatment of Chronic Disease.Vol 2. The Science Department of Pascoe Pharmazeutische Pr_parateGmbH (Giessen)5th Revised Edition 1990

hands-free sets; some research considers that these give no protection, whilst others speak of a "significant level of protection". Our own findings confirm this: some sets reduce the problem and others seemingly make no difference at all.

Whilst there are many factors involved with cancer, we have often found that once the problem of electromagnetic fields is addressed, palliative care changes into curative care.

A fair amount of research has been carried out into the affects of mobile phones. Biologist Roger Coghill suggested that the microwaves generated by mobile phones have the ability to damage white blood cells, which play a vital role in the body's immune system. A BBC report stated that:

> *"Mr Coghill claims the body's immune system is partially controlled by electromagnetic fields emitted by the body. He believes the radiation emitted by mobile phones damages the body's own electromagnetic fields, and undermines the proper functioning of the immune system. In this report he said that there was no harm using mobile phones for two or three minutes. But people who left them on for 20 minutes or more could be doing themselves harm."*
>
> *BBC News, 15th Oct 1998*

In the past, researchers have thought that the main damage to cells from microwaves and radiowaves was due to the thermal energy they produce, which was thought to damage the functioning of the cells by heating them up. Research however has found that the heat produced is not great enough to cause cell damage. However, EM signalling is the primary means of communication between cells. Therefore we are fundamentally electromagnetic beings and consequently we can be affected by external EMFs.

In Europe, cattle grazing in fields near mobile masts started behaving strangely after the installation of macrocell antennae. Their milk yields were way down, spontaneous abortions were up and older cows were dying[36].

Dr Gerald Hyland of Warwick University believes, that an unrecognisable hazard of mobiles is that, in the more modern systems, the EM signals are not sent out continuously like radiowaves, but in pulses. This pulsed transmission is a particular feature of the GSM (global system for mobiles) technology. These pulse rates, says Dr Hyland, can have serious biological effects:

"The pulses happen to be close to some of the brain's own electrical and electrochemical rhythms. Since these are involved in the control and regulation of bioprocesses essential for well-being, it is reasonable to anticipate that the functionality of the body will be impaired"

'Lancet', 2000;356: 1833-6

Currently technology is still rapidly progressing; the third generation phone or '3G' phone allows internet access but also operate in GSM/2G mode at times. However, in 'New Scientist' October 2003, Duncan Graham-Rowe reported that "Exposure to radio signals from 3G cell-phone base stations can cause headaches and nausea". The study compared GSM (Global System for Mobiles) phone signals to 3G signals on the cognitive signals of 36 volunteers. Their findings were that:

"They found a significant relationship between exposure to the 3G signal and detrimental effects on general 'well-being', characterised by feelings of nausea, tingling and headaches. No relationships were found for GSM exposure. Both 3G and GSM signals affected cognitive functions in some cases, including reaction times, memory and alertness."[37]

Most people are generally aware that mobile phones are bad for them; however it is less well known that cordless phones and their base stations are as bad or even worse! We have found numerous patients suffering from elec-

36 Pract Vet Sur, 1998; 79:437-44
37 www.newscientist.com/news/news.jsp?id=ns99994225

tromagnetic stress and it is only upon doing home visits that we have found that they often have a phone base station in their bedroom, and often on the bedside table. With the use of an electrosmog detector (sensory perception, Swiss Shield), we pinpointed that these base stations are a big cause of electromagnetic stress. Wireless DECT phones (Digital Enhanced Cordless Telephones), like mobiles phones, work with pulse modulation. However, a major difference between them is that DECT phones not only transmit whilst you are making a phone call, they do so all day long whether you are using them or not[38]. Many models do not adjust their power level, as most 2G & 3G phones will, therefore they are emitting radiation 24 hours a day, making them even more harmful than mobile phones![39].

WI-FI NETWORKS (& INTERNET ACCESS)

Wi-fi is another addition to our already electro-polluted environment and as Britain has undergone a Wi-Fi revolution with offices, homes and classrooms going wireless, there is concern that the technology could carry health risks.

Wi-fi works by transmitting information via radio waves from a wired network to a computer. Researchers for BBC's Panorama programme found that the maximum signal strength was three times higher than that of a typical mobile phone mast[40]. There are already calls for inquiries to be made into the long-term health affects of the use of wi-fi.

BLUE-TOOTH

Blue tooth is a short range, low power wireless data connectivity designed to allow an enormous range of devices

38 Some low radiation DECT phones (for instance by Orchid) run at lowest power and do stop transmissions when there is no call. Check the phone stops when there is no call whether or not it is docked on the base station.

39 Daily Mail, 12th June 2006

40 Daily Mail, May 21st 2007

to communicate with each other. It is a cheap technology and thus is in many digital devices as well as computers, phones and cars. It is a pulsed microwave and will often be continuously transmitting unless switched off.

SUMMARY OF WIRELESS DATA TECHNOLOGIES

This is a rapidly moving area of technology with great attractions to many users – particularly the young who may also be the most at risk. The technologies inevitably involve international standards and large commercial vested interests, while independent health research into the effects lags far behind the proliferation of the technologies. Epidemiological evidence takes many years to accumulate and, as with ELF near power lines, takes many further years to gain enough clarity and significance to be widely accepted.

Interestingly there is evidence that birds may be highly susceptible. It may be no coincidence that the large decline in urban sparrows happens along with the introduction of ubiquitous urban cell and wi-fi technologies.

You can read considerable information on all these technologies and their relative risks and merits on the internet. Apart from the direct power level being received by your body, which can cause slight heating effects, there are much stronger concerns about the impacts of the complex modulation, phasing and pulsing nature of signals. One useful resource on signal issues is www.powerwatch.org.uk/science/pulse.asp, but there are many you can easily find.

Which are likely to have the greatest impact on you depends on the technology, duration of exposure, relative location of devices and method of use (eg handset or hands-free).

LOW-ENERGY BULBS AND FLAT SCREEN TELEVISIONS

Recently we found on several home visits that patients were sensitive when a low energy light bulb was switched on. Upon questioning we discovered that in a lot of cases their symptoms had only come on since they had switched their bulbs to energy-saving ones.

The charity Epilepsy Action reports that "those with the condition are complaining of dizziness, loss of focus and discomfort after being exposed to light from the energy-saving bulbs". This is of great concern since the UK government has agreed to phase out the old-fashioned, incandescent bulbs.

As to why they are having this affect is undecided, but it is thought that it may be due to different wavelength pattern generated by the bulbs. Or it could be due to the fact that low energy bulbs produce a much higher electromagnetic field than tungsten bulbs. More research is needed in this area, as although it is important that we conserve the world's resources, these energy-saving bulbs appear to be detrimental to our health.

A case that we have seen is a child's eczema, which seemed to be well under control, but which flared up when he stayed at his grandmother's house. She had recently installed low-energy bulbs. When the bulbs were changed back to conventional ones, the eczema cleared up. However, we have found that halogen energy saving bulbs do not seem to be detrimental to health

There are in existence different kinds of low energy bulbs. The halogen bulb offers less saving on the traditional bulb than some others do, but nevertheless, at 30% reduction in electricity consumption, the reduction is significant. The Halogen bulb is, in our experience, the least problematic of low energy bulbs currently in production, at any rate in respect of electromagnetic fields. It may be that the future will soon lie with LED (Light Emitting Diode) bulbs, which contain no hazardous halogen or mercury. These consume a very small amount of current and could therefore be expected to emit a correspondingly small electromagnetic field, although the authors are not yet in a position to verify this from clinical findings. The disadvantage of LED bulbs currently lies in their high production costs, though these may perhaps fall when and if they attain widespread usage.

We have also had similar findings with flat screen televisions. Upon muscle testing we have found some people weakened when a flat screen television is plugged in, even if only on stand-by. One case involved a 4 year old boy suffering from asthma who used to regularly play in front of the television in the living room, his bedroom was also directly above. After a protective device, an Elo-Rayex (see Appendix 7) was put in place his asthma cleared up.

TYPES AND SOURCES OF ELECTROMAGNETIC STRESS

An alternating electric field is present in any cable which is simply plugged in to the mains, even if it's not switched on. Therefore in the home we are permanently being exposed to these electric fields even when appliances aren't actually switched on. This needs to be thought of especially with regards to sleeping, which is when you are most suspectible to noxious influences, as well as being such a large part of your life. Cables running under the bed or behind the headboard will emit an electric field, which may be amplified if you have a mattress containing metal springs[41]. A lot of bedrooms contain a bed with bedside lamp either side; in this situation there is most likely an electrical cable lying in the wall at the head of the bed, within a very short distance of where your head will spend a large part of its day!

Electric blankets are particularly hazardous as they produce an electric field, which has been measured at 2,000V/m, and which is within a cm of your body! These are the worst field generators to be found in the bedroom.

Alternating magnetic fields are produced when power flows, i.e. when the appliance is switched on. Our houses are filled with these electromagnetic fields, which are

41 'Bio-Resonance According to Paul Schmidt' by Dietmar Heimes.2004

doing untold damage to us. We have been surprised at the number of patients who are sensitive to their plug-in alarm clocks, which seem fairly harmless appliances. However, they contain a transformer which changes the high 240 volts mains input to the required 5 volts. The transformer results in a surprisingly large alternating magnetic frequency – 100mT within a 2m range. Most electronic gadgets contain transformers.

Generally the rule is that if you double the distance, then you quarter the burden. In short, all electrical cables and appliances need to be kept at a distance.

Continuous electric fields are created when a person wears synthetic clothing which in turn generates static electricity. We have found in our clinics that a number of people are sensitive to the clothing that they are wearing – from dresses and jumpers to socks, shoes and underpants. We have even found some patients being weakened from the synthetic hair tie they are wearing. To avoid this type of continuous electric field, fabrics made of natural materials, such as cotton or linen, should be used, and leather-soled shoes instead of man-made. We have also found children who are sensitive to their stuffed toys, made with synthetic fur, which they are often sleeping next to.

HYBRID VEHICLES

Concern currently exists over the dangers of magnetic fields in hybrid vehicles, albeit that such health risks are denied by the manufacturers. Once again, it is a question of what level of electromagnetism should be considered to be harmless. Safety levels will vary from person to person but, in our experience, are regularly found to be significantly lower than those currently averred by official wisdom. As in the case of low energy light bulbs, the authors welcome any technical developments from the standpoint of reduction in fossil fuel consumption, a vitally important subject for the future of the planet, but naturally choose to view the topic from all angles. Fortunately, it appears possible to obtain protection from such fields.

PROTECTION AGAINST ELECTROMAGNETIC STRESS

We live in an increasingly high-tech world. There is no going back and some have claimed that we have turned our environment into something akin to a nuclear power-station. Even if we use few electrical appliances ourselves, we are unable to go into any public place without finding people near us using their mobile phones. If we travel by train (from which we receive electromagnetic stress), the chances are that we will be sitting next to someone who is using a mobile phone. So what simple measures can we take?

LIMITING OUR EXPOSURE TO ELECTROMAGNETIC FIELDS

Electrical equipment which is plugged in, even if not switched on, can expose us to harmful electromagnetic fields. One of the best examples is an electric blanket. The worst type is an over blanket that is designed to be left on all night, but an under blanket can still be harmful if it is left plugged in, even though switched off. On retiring, the plug should be pulled out of the socket. It is also not advisable to sleep within about 1.5 metres of a mains-operated clock radio. Similarly, whenever possible, keep the same distance away from electric ovens, microwave ovens and other electronic equipment. As more radiation is emitted from the back of a television than from the front, take care that neither your bed, nor your favourite armchair, is directly behind it.

In the home, most EMF exposure comes from buried electrical wiring. It is best to check areas where a lot of time is spent – for most people this would include the bed.

DEGAUSSING

Whilst there are ways to protect ourselves, sometimes we need to rectify what has happened to our bodies and their electrical circuits. One method is by degaussing, or demagnetising. This procedure is commonly applied to electronic objects, and, during the last World War, many ships were treated to prevent them from attracting floating mines owing to their electronic polarity. If they were about to hit a mine head-on, the degaussing caused them to repel the mine, thus preventing disaster. We have also heard stories that fishing boats are degaussed in order to prevent them from attracting sea-borne debris and to ensure that their nets keep clear of the hulls. Electricians degauss music systems to remove the 'hum', and televisions to improve the picture quality and eliminate static. Some computers have a degaussing button for a similar purpose.

To degauss people may seem a little unorthodox, as we cannot hear the 'hum' or see a poor picture quality, but our muscles and brains work by electrical impulses. We are 'electrical beings', and stories are now appearing on the Internet about the success of degaussing people.

WHO CAN IT HELP?

This will probably help if you:

- are affected by power lines, computers, etc.
- get frequent static electric shocks
- 'interfere' with radios, battery watches, etc., causing them to malfunction
- are 'addicted' to television or computer games
- live or work in an area of geopathic stress

HOW DO I DO IT?

An electric hairdryer can be used to degauss (demagnetise) the body. Switch on and then run the back of the dryer up and down the body. Note this is the opposite to the way most people use a hairdryer. The air is blowing away from you, but it is the electric motor which is doing the job and the heat can be switched off. If you use a hairdryer to dry your hair, just turn it around for a few seconds afterwards. This needs to be done at least once a week, or more frequently (such as 3 times a day) for anyone who is particularly sensitive electrically. The whole procedure takes just a few seconds. Keep a hairdryer in your bedroom, and whenever you go in just switch it on and run the back up and down the body. It is impossible to do this too often and it only takes a few seconds each time.

Degaussing can be performed with any piece of electrical equipment containing a motor and a magnet. The advantage of using a hairdryer is that, firstly, it was designed to be held in the hand and, secondly, if the hairdryer is symmetrical (i.e. the motor is not on one side), and most are, then it is the back of it that nearly always demagnetises. It may sound weird – but it works!

For example, whilst lecturing we came across a student who was incredibly sensitive to electromagnetic fields. She was affected by mobile phones and halogen lights, and had not been able to go into the cities to shop for the last 5 years. She was desensitised to the electromagnetic stress and told to de-gausse (de-magnetize). A few months later she wrote to thank us "for bringing life back to normality".

A colleague was suffering from eczema and had been to various practitioners with resulting improvements in her energy and well being, but no change in her skin. She complained of feeling tired after using her computer, of feeling ill after visiting an acupuncturist who used electric needles, and of continually experiencing static shocks when getting out of her car. She was advised to degauss herself three times daily for just a few seconds each time – therefore for less than about 15 seconds a day – and within a week the long-standing eczema had healed. We have also seen many cases of Irritable Bowel Syndrome cured thus, but only, of course, when the maintaining cause was suspected and confirmed to be electromagnetic fields.

IS IT DANGEROUS?

Some people are anxious about using a hairdryer because they have been told that they should reduce their exposure to electrical equipment as much as possible. However, here the alternating magnetic pole of the hairdryer motor is being used to demagnetise the body and so make it less susceptible to electromagnetic pollution.

PROTECTIVE DEVICES

In many of our cases it was noticed that the symptoms returned if degaussing was neglected for any significant period. An analogy we sometimes use is that of a coal miner going to the coalface and getting covered in coal dust. The equivalent of the coalface may be the computer, the vacuum cleaner or simply the radio mast near to where you live. The miner will wash off the dust with soap and water, and degaussing is the equivalent of this action. Yet the miner knows that the next time he goes to the coalface his skin will once again be covered in dust – unless, of course, he wears protective clothing. He must, however, still wash himself, because a small amount of coal dust will have passed through the seams of his clothing on to his skin, but not nearly as much as without the protective suit. Therefore regular degaussing is essential in sensitive individuals.

HOW CAN I FIND OUT MORE?

Try reading '*Geopathic Stress: How Earth Energies Affect Our Lives*' by Jane Thurnell-Rea.

TOURMALINE

One of the simplest things to use, and perhaps the cheapest, is the mineral tourmaline. This either deflects or absorbs electromagnetic fields. A piece of tourmaline placed on a computer, microwave oven or mobile phone significantly reduces the harmful effects of electromagnetic fields. Tourmaline jewellery provides the same benefits to the wearer.

Tourmaline is rich in piezoelectric and pyroelectric properties. Piezoelectricity was first discovered in quartz crystals. This effect allows them to be used in certain sorts of radio tuners (first done in 1921, but now largely replaced by other types), in the timing mechanisms of quartz watches, and in the electronics industry. Tourmaline, another strongly piezoelectric mineral, is used in gauges to measure transient blast pressures. If worn, it needs to be rinsed regularly, perhaps daily, because of the build-up of static impeding its action.

USING HANDS-FREE PHONES

When using a mobile phone the levels of radiation that you are exposed to can be reduced by using a hands-free kit. Wireless Bluetooth headsets can pick up signals to the phone up to 10 metres away. Tests have shown that this reduces the radiation to the head by up to 90 percent[42]. Mobile phones transmit at maximum power when turning them on and off, and also when connecting and disconnecting. Therefore it is best to keep the handset away from your ear when dialling out[43]. Also hold the phone away from you when sending a text and keep the mobile away from the body as much as possible, i.e. not in your pocket. Avoid using a mobile phone for long periods of time; Dietmar Heimes recommends no longer than 2 minutes. Also, when talking, if possible use the loudspeaker facility on your phone so that the phone does not have to be close to the ear.

42 'Evening Standard' 11th Jan 2005
43 'The Powerwatch Handbook', Alasdair and Jean Philips

DESENSITISATION

Acupressure points (see Appendix 2) can also stimulate the immune system and strengthen it against electricity. Here a mobile phone and/or a battery operated device could be placed on CV6.

COLOURED LIGHT

Blue and green light can also offer protection against electromagnetic stress (see Chapter 8).

COPPER COINS

Environmental electricians are aware that copper is very good at absorbing various frequencies, because it is a super conductor. Placing a couple of pre-1992 copper coins, 1p or 2p, near to a computer monitor and screen stops the computer having a detrimental affect on the patient. A penny coin stuck to a mobile phone also seems to be protective. We have also experimented with placing copper coins around bed mattresses and found them to counteract the induction in the metal springs.

Please note that since 1992 UK copper coins have only a nominal amount of copper in them, due to the cost of copper, and therefore offer no protection.

A man suffering from Crohn's disease was discovered to have metal toxicity from an ear-ring. He went into remission for a year after removal of the ear-ring. However, it then came back when he got a new girlfriend whose place he was staying at about three times a week. Upon questioning it was discovered that there was a phone charger near her bed: it was recommended that he put a 2p coin on the charger, which he did each time he visited and this led to his symptoms clearing up.

[Note: we do not advocate the use of copper bracelets, as these generally in turn become a maintaining cause – see Chapter 9 on metals.]

ELO-RAYEX

A much more sophisticated version of the copper coins is a German designed device called the Elo-Rayex which has been specifically developed to reduce or eliminate the negative radiation in the electrical system in the house or office (see Appendix 7). It works by being placed on the house fuse box. We have found through testing that it dramatically reduces the weakening affects caused by base stations, phone charges, computers, car key fobs, etc.

An office manager placed an Elo-Rayex on the fuse box of the office. Subsequently the amount of sick leave went down and she noticed that less people were complaining about headaches at the end of the day. A 36yr old lady who had had a persistent cough for several months found that it cleared up after she had put an Elo-Rayex on her fuse box. A child always developed itchy skin whilst being driven somewhere in the car. An Elo-Rayex, placed on the dash board during the journey, stopped the itching. A 40 year old female had persistent sore throats and ear problems. We found that she was being affected by a satellite dish. An Elo-Rayex on the fuse box helped clear up these health problems.

MINI-RAYONEX

The mini-Rayonex is similar to the Elo-Rayex, but is smaller and is designed to be portable. It contains one aerial which offers protection from the most common harmful frequency. This can be carried around in a bag or pocket and offers protection outside the home.

The World Health Organisation (WHO) calls the electronic smog one of the most common and fastest growing environmental influences and stresses that it takes seriously concerns about the possible health effects. It adds that everyone in the world is exposed to it and that "levels will continue to increase as technology advances"[44].

44 'The Independent on Sunday', 7th May 2006

CHAPTER 8

GEOPATHIC STRESS AND COLOURED LIGHT

Geopathic stress or Black Streams have been found to be a common factor in illnesses and psychological conditions, much like electromagnetic stress. Black Streams are a form of geological stress and can be anything from a few centimetres to many metres wide. They lie where natural vibrations from inside the Earth, which are at about 8Hz (cycles per second), ascend from the centre of the Earth and are distorted by certain obstacles such as subterranean running water, mineral concentrations, fault lines or underground cavities. As this energy ascends, its natural wavelength can be altered, changing its frequency to up to 250Hz. These high frequency vibrations are harmful to living organisms and are known as geopathic stress.

Geopathic stress is not the direct cause of illness, but illness:

> *"develops as a result of the breakdown of the body's natural functioning and lowering of the immune system"*[45].

Dr Hulda Clark theorizes that perhaps it is the changed electrical charge or magnetic force of damaged organs that permits further development of the fluke stages of parasites:

> *"Perhaps it is merely low immune surveillance. Perhaps the dying cells of a damaged organ provide food for the baby stages. Only further scientific study will reveal the truth."*

This seems to closely parallel George Vithoulkas' theorization in his book, 'New Model for Health and Disease', where he writes about the possibility that:

> *".... after a stressor's encounter with an organism, conditions can develop within the system which might allow the*

45 'Are You Sleeping in a Safe Place?', Rolf Gordon

mutation of innocuous micro-organisms into ones which can cause pathology? ... [that diseases,] must have an underlying, continuing cause which is not the bacteria, virus or fungus but the deep-seated predisposition of the organism".

In his book, Rolf Gordon tells the story of 15-year-old Linda.

"Linda was diagnosed with leukaemia, went through chemotherapy and bone marrow replacement. In November 1984 she was discharged from the hospital and at home she first slept in her mother's bed. Her recovery was steady. In March 1985 Linda moved back to her old bed and in a follow-up a little later the leukaemia showed itself again. The doctors wanted to act at once, but a friend of the family told Linda and her family about Black Streams. Linda's room was examined and the results showed that she could not have slept in a worse place as Black Streams crossed right under her bed. The bed was moved. In April, Linda went for another follow-up and doctors decided to wait and see. Her recovery continued and some months later she was well again".[46]

AUSTRIAN RESEARCH

Both Valdimarsson and Gordon refer to the 'Austrian Working Party for Research into Geopathic Stress Sites' led by Dr Otto Bergmann, Professor at Vienne University[47]. Tests were carried out on 985 people over two years. The volunteers were asked to sit on chairs for ten minutes without knowing that they were sitting in a geopathic stress zone. They were subject to:

"medical examination both before and after the test, including blood sedimentation tests, measuring of electric conductance of certain muscle points, of blood pressure, heart beat, breathing, skin resistance and blood circulation.

46 Gordon, R. Are You Sleeping In A Safe Place? Dulwich Health (London). 6th Edition 1999. p.12 [5]

47 Morgunbla□i□,Valdimarsson, Valdimar: lecture in the Nordic House 29.4.'97

462,421 measurements were taken in 6,943 individual tests. Although the people tested were exposed to geopathic stress for only a few minutes, the harmful effect could be registered in most cases."

One can imagine the dire consequences which exposure to geopathic stress over many years could have.

According to Rolf Gordon it has been shown that:

"resistance to treatment, including slow or partial recovery.... is connected with the presence of Geopathic Stress and, when its influence is removed, a spontaneous improvement in health occurs as the treatment starts to take effect"

Geopathic stress can therefore be a maintaining cause of a disease, since it develops as a result of the breakdown of the body's natural functioning and lowering of the immune system.

Environmental pollution is an increasing factor in our lives. Jane Thurnell-Read describes the human body as a bucket that fills with a certain amount of water whenever a person is stressed by an environmental pollution factor. Symptoms occur when the bucket overflows, but it is impossible to say that any one factor is the cause of the disease, for "it is the sum total of all the factors that pushes the person over the threshold into illness".[48] Therefore, it is of the utmost importance to clear away, as much as possible, the most harmful factors, such as electromagnetic and geopathic stress.

We suspect that the presence of electromagnetic stress is what can make us more sensitive to geopathic stress.

PROTECTION AND DEALING WITH GEOPATHIC STRESS

Copper again is a very good insulator against these noxious frequencies and absorbs the ascending frequencies. Therefore we recommend that people affected by this stress place copper coins in the areas affected.

Desensitising the patient to the problem is also very beneficial (see Appendix 2). In this technique, a vial

48 Thurnell-Read,J. Geopathic Stress: How Earth Energies Affect Our Lives

which has been exposed to the geopathic stress frequency, is placed on CV6. This can significantly improve the body's ability to cope with the effects of geopathic stress.

The Raditech multiwave oscillator, developed by Rolf Gordon and sold by Dulwich Health, brings the high vibration caused by geopathic stress down to the earth's natural vibration of around 8Hz. Their publicity brochure states that the Raditech incorporates electronics, powerful magnets and cables, and can be used in flats and houses. It is plugged into the ring main, but uses little electricity and will clear geopathic stress within a short time, simply by the person putting his feet on it. Reactions from people who have installed a Raditech include:

"My backache – migraine – PMS pains – asthma – allergy disappeared."

"We now talk together. My son of 23 became such a pleasant boy overnight."

"My child stopped crying – bedwetting – being hyperactive etc."

Horse owner – "My pony refused to go into my new stables until I had installed a Raditech."

COLOURED LIGHTS

Finally we have discovered a cheap, yet very effective way of reducing both electromagnetic and geopathic stress: different coloured lights.

As a result of research in Ireland, we learned that geopathic stress vibrations have a certain frequency which happen to be interfered with by the frequency of red or pink light. Consequently the negative effects of geopathic stress can be counteracted by red or pink light. We have found that having a low wattage red light bulb in a geopathically stressed room reduces the geopathic stress significantly in that room. As geopathic stress comes from the earth upwards, a red light in a downstairs room will also negate the stress in the room above. However, the reverse does not work: a red light upstairs will not affect the room below.

An elderly patient recently came in suffering from geopathic stress. Upon testing her in her home, geopathic stress was found throughout her house, with the exception of one room. Upon investigation, the lack of geopathic stress in this room was attributed to the fact that she had an artificial coal fire in the room which was emitting red light, thereby negating its effects. A red light in her bedroom slowly eliminated abdominal pains. Another woman always awoke with headaches. To her surprise this did not happen over the Christmas period. Investigation showed her bed to be in a geopathically stressed area, and over Christmas she had red lights from the Christmas tree shining into her room.

Similarly, electromagnetic stress can be counteracted with blue light. We have found that people who are affected by a mobile phone or when sitting in front of a computer are not so affected when a blue light is introduced into the room. Therefore we recommend to people who have computers or an office at home that they put a blue light in their room.

A flight controller at an international airport was suffering from asthma; he was being significantly affected by the computers around him. A small blue light in the control tower dramatically improved his breathing.

A woman living near a radio mast was suffering from menopausal problems and tiredness caused by her environment. In her kitchen and living room she put a daylight bulb (which has the full light spectrum), and in her bedroom, which was closest to the mast, she put a small 5 watt blue Christmas tree-like bulb. She also de-gaussed and her problems all cleared up within a few weeks. We have found daylight bulbs to be very advantageous as they contain the red, blue and green frequencies, unlike a normal light bulb. They are not full spectrum in that they do not seem to emit the yellow frequency, but are very different to being out in the sunshine in that the individual frequencies are there as if through a prism, and there is the obvious advantage that one can see clearly with the aid of them.

Green bulbs can be very useful with the problems created by Wi-fi systems and hand-held computer games; we have found these linked into hypo-, hyper-activity, tiredness and headaches.

We have found yellow light to be beneficial in neutralising harmful effects from magnetic appliances, flat screen televisions and low energy bulbs. The fashion for magnetic pillows, mattresses, insoles etc can be helpful for a while, but prolonged use may affect the magnetic polarity of the body. Security passes also contain a magnetic strip and often people can be wearing these all day at work without being aware of the detrimental effect they can be having on them. These effects can be reduced by de-gaussing, the use of a yellow light or simply avoiding the use of these items. A yellow light was also discovered to be beneficial for a baby suffering from colic. Upon a house visit the yellow light was necessary due to the fact that the baby was sensitive to the baby monitor that was next to her bed. The yellow light negated the detrimental affects of the frequencies produced by this monitor and the colic cleared up.

HOW CAN THIS POSSIBLY WORK?

As we are electromagnetic beings with our own frequencies, we are greatly affected by frequencies surrounding us, be it from other people or from our environment. Certain frequencies will resonate[49] with our own natural frequency and in these instances the affects will be beneficial and will help optimise our health. This is similar to

49 Imagine six pendulums hung next to one another, all different lengths except for two. They are all stationary, then one of these two same length pendulums is swung; the pendulum of matching length will start to swing, whilst the others will not. This is because the two matching pendulums have the same frequency, resulting in harmonious swinging: this is resonance.

the action of homœopathic remedies. However, frequencies caused by geopathic and electromagnetic stress do not resonate with our bodily frequencies and actually throw them out of cycle, causing a lowering of our tolerance and weakening the body's natural defence systems. This is simply demonstrated by looking back to the days when television screens were affected by someone vacuum cleaning nearby; the frequency of the vacuum cleaner disturbed the frequency of the TV signal, causing a fuzzy picture.

As we go through the electromagnetic spectrum we have varying frequencies of radio waves, then infrared, then the visible light spectrum (red, orange, yellow, green, blue, indigo and violet), ultra-violet, microwaves and gamma rays, starting with the lowest frequency to the highest respectively. Some of these frequencies have been found to neutralise other similar frequencies. The colours with lower frequencies such as red and pink (but not orange or the fire-glow bulbs) will negate the harmful effects of geopathic stress. Whilst at the other end of the visible light frequency, blue will neutralise the harmful effects caused by electromagnetic stress.

In the middle, a green light will be beneficial if someone is being affected by the frequency of battery-operated appliances, phone chargers and base stations. Yellow is good if someone is over-magnetised. The wearing of these colours will have little effect, but if they are transmitted in the form of light the results can be far-reaching.

So often hypo- or hyper-activity in children or adults is caused by the affect of environmental electricity on the electricity of the brain. We have seen appropriate coloured light bulbs negate the need for drugs and improve sleep, anxiety levels, concentration and energy as well as other physical conditions.

A teenage boy suffering from Attention Deficit Disorder spent every evening playing computer games.

Once his family had put a daylight bulb in the area where he played the games he began to sleep better and his teacher commented that his concentration had also improved. In the room where he played was a Wi-fi station, so the use of a daylight bulb containing the green frequency neutralised the effects from the Gameboy and the frequency from the Wi-fi.

A pink or red, green, yellow or blue bulb, according to need, does not have to be shining brightly. A small 15 watt bulb is adequate, which of course only needs to be shining when a person is in the room. Even in daylight it will make all the difference. It does not need to turn the room a different colour, and the subject does not even need to be aware of it. What the light does to the frequency in the room is what matters – people do not even have to realise that it is on.

SUMMARY

Where geopathic stress is found, use a pink, red or daylight bulb to neutralise the area. When operating battery powered appliances or toys, base stations, wi-fi and phone chargers, a green light will be beneficial. This can be very helpful for certain children. Yellow light is useful for people who are over-magnetised or have been overexposed to low energy light bulbs. Finally, where there are televisions, computers and similar devices such as photocopiers and fax machines, a blue or daylight bulb is necessary. These can be bought or ordered from most electrical shops. Daylight bulbs can also often be bought from art and craft shops.

Where there is doubt or a mixture of frequencies, invest in a daylight bulb.

As research is ongoing the authors would value hearing of any experiences which would add to the assimilation of data.

CHAPTER 9

METALS

The next area that we will consider, and which is one of the most common causes of health problems, is that of metals. There are three main reasons for this which we regularly come across, or it can be a mixture of these factors. Firstly, the problem could be that of mercury amalgam fillings which may be getting old and leaking, and to which the person is sensitive. Secondly, there may be metals that someone is working with, or coming into frequent contact with, which are causing a problem. And thirdly, there may be metals that someone is wearing which need investigation. Furthermore we can subdivide the problem into two categories – metals that are being worn and absorbed through the skin, and metals that are acting as aerials or conductors for electromagnetic stress.

MERCURY AMALGAM

The Greeks called mercury 'watersilver'. Although they knew it to be very dangerous, its usefulness – particularly as an antiseptic – was also well known. It was widely used in the battle against syphilis. Because of its solvent quality, and because it is a great conductor of electricity, mercury is used in the electrical industry (batteries) and in laboratories. It is found in lead automobile and industrial exhausts, in power plants, water pipes, some thermometers, certain vaccines, eye drops and antibiotics.

The word amalgam comes from the Arabic 'al malgham', which means emollient or curative lotion. Its use in dentistry started in Paris in 1826, when M. Taveau mixed together half mercury and half silver. Modern amalgam fillings are different from the original formula. Instead of just silver, more metals are mixed together, e.g. copper, tin, thallium, nickel, chromium, and zinc. The blend can vary, but what has not changed is that mercury makes up 50% of the amalgam filling.

The Icelandic dentist Jón Börkur Árnason, wrote a newspaper article about a report issued in 1991 by the World Health Organisation (WHO). In this report it is stated that virtually everybody in Iceland is exposed to mercury from amalgam fillings. Every 24 hours approximately 3 – 17mcg of mercury vapours releases from the fillings, and 2 – 3mcg of methyl mercury is ingested from fish and seafood[50].

Another Icelandic dentist, Árni Jónsson, points out the hypocrisy of saying that amalgam is so 'dangerously toxic' that it cannot be released into the Atlantic Ocean, but that it is alright to put it in people's teeth. He also points out that dentists are ordered to use special equipment in order to stop amalgam from spreading into the atmosphere because of its toxicity. He states that it is an undeniable fact that mercury gradually releases from amalgam fillings and settles in organs such as the brain, the nervous system, pituitary gland and kidneys. The main argument is not about that, but about whether it can damage the functioning of the body. He claims that most scientists admit that it can damage 'some' people. Of course people's susceptibility differs, but why do we have to take the risk, and what justifies it?

Dr Hajikakou, who runs a homœopathic amalgam-free dental practice in East Sussex, UK, observes:

> *It is ironic that waste amalgam (i.e. outside the body) must be stored in secure conditions owing to the release of mercury vapour and has to be disposed of by licensed disposal companies. However, when it is placed in people's teeth it "miraculously" transforms itself into a completely inert material, which is perfectly safe! At least that is the official line. It is generally agreed that if amalgam was introduced today as a restorative material, it would never pass FDA (Food and Drug Administration) approval. The case against using amalgam is, in my opinion, overwhelming*[51].

50 Morgunbla□i□, Jón B_rkur Àrnason 10th August 1998

51 The full text of Dr Hajikakou's article appears in Appendix 9

In a newspaper interview Irene Hostler, a former dentist from Wymondham near Norwich, describes how her whole family was poisoned with mercury. She says that as a student she had not been told that routine exposure to dental amalgam could cause mercury toxicity. She was told that mercury was dangerous, but she understood that people would need massive exposure. She was also told that once mercury was mixed with other metals in the amalgam it was 'locked in' and safe[52].

Sweden has led the way in researching mercury poisoning and has taken action against the use of amalgam. In 1987 the governments of Sweden and Germany issued warnings against the use of amalgam with pregnant women and children. In 1994 its use for children and adolescents under 19 years was banned in Sweden, and for the rest of the population on 1st January 1997. The German Department of Health has repeated its warning against amalgam use for children and pregnant women, and has banned the use of certain types of amalgam for the whole population[53].

Several studies have evaluated the health effects of replacing mercury-containing dental fillings with non-mercury substitutes. Research showed that symptoms of mercury poisoning have a wide range. The most common symptoms were fatigue, depression, dizziness, headaches, skin disturbances, vision problems and metallic taste. The main question is not whether the patient is allergic to dental amalgam, but rather the direct causal relationship of amalgam fillings to the development of allergies to food, chemicals and environmental factors.

In his book *'The Toxic Time Bomb'*, Sam Ziff describes how our saliva is full of metal ions, which means it is an electrolyte and can transport or conduct electrical current from one point to another; and the oxygen in our mouths can cause metal to give up electrons. Thus, when an

52 'Daily Mail', 2nd May 2000
53 'The Toxic Time Bomb' Ziff pp. 204-5

amalgam filling is installed in a tooth, it is subjected to all the chemicals in the mouth, which start wearing away the amalgam. Sam Ziff cites much research which shows substantial loss of mercury from amalgam fillings over time.

This raises the question as to whether the mercury we swallow is a factor in nutritional deficit or metabolic impairment. In an article, J.G. Levenson states,

> *"when the mercury vapour enters the saliva in people's mouths and is swallowed, it will combine with hydrochloric acid to form mercuric chloride ... [which] ... will destroy gut bacteria and allow an overgrowth of candida and other yeasts. The formation of this compound may leave the body deficient in hydrochloric acid, thus digestion is not correctly initiated and cannot proceed efficiently"*[54].

Jón Börkur Árnason quotes the Swedish Medical Journal[55], which published detailed results of research by two scientists in the Swedish Working Environment Institute (Arbetsmiljöinstitutet) that measured mercury in urine and stools from people who had amalgam fillings and from people who had none. The results proved that there is a direct link between the amount of amalgam fillings in the teeth and the amount of mercury measured in stools. In the person who had the most fillings, 190mcg of mercury was found in his stools every 24 hours, while the one with no fillings measured at 1.8mcg. These results stirred up great interest and were widely discussed in the Swedish media, mostly because of the strict scientific methods that were used[56].

A kinesiology test will show whether the patient needs to have one or more fillings changed. A bottle containing amalgam filling is placed near the patient's mouth, the muscle is then tested (see Appendix 2) and, if it weakens, amalgam poisoning is likely to be the cause of their problem. It won't necessarily be all the fillings that are leaking, so, in order to check, the practitioner places a tissue

54 'Nutrition and Amalgam Filling', Felmore Ltd. Health Publications no 149
55 Lakartidningen nr. 15 1992
56 Morgunbla□i□, 10th August 1998

over his finger, touches one filling and tests the muscle at the same time. This has to be done with all the fillings in order to decide how many need to be replaced by another material. In his special chapter in the book *'Menace in the Mouth'*, Dr. Robert Hempleman explains how he uses Applied Kinesiology to diagnose amalgam leakage in dentistry.

Having amalgam fillings replaced with composite ones can cause temporary problems if some of the amalgam is released into the body. The use of a rubber dam by the dentist will significantly reduce the possibilities of problems. In our experience, people who have had mercury extracted may have experienced an exacerbation of their problem for a few weeks – after which improvement sets in. The use of the homœopathic remedy Hepar Sulphuris will often help reduce symptoms. Other methods of treating metal toxicity are discussed by Dr Hajikakou in his article (see Appendix 10).

Research done in 1989 on 285 patients who complained about joint and muscle pain, and then had their fillings changed, showed that 213 of them felt much better afterwards. This would indicate that there is a strong link between amalgam and symptoms of poisoning.

SELECTED HEALTH SYMPTOM ANALYSIS[57]

% of total	Reporting symptom	Cases	Cases improved or cured	% cure/ improved
14%	Allergy	221	196	89%
5%	Anxiety	86	80	93%
5%	Bad temper	81	68	89%
6%	Bloating	88	70	88%
6%	Blood pressure	99	53	54%
5%	Chest pains	79	69	87%
22%	Depression	347	315	91%
22%	Dizziness	343	301	88%
45%	Fatigue	705	603	86%
15%	Gastrointestinal problems	231	192	83%
8%	Gum problems	129	121	94%
34%	Headaches	531	460	87%
3%	Migraine	45	39	87%
12%	Insomnia	187	146	78%
10%	Irregular heartbeat	159	139	87%
8%	Irritability	132	119	90%
17%	Poor concentration	270	216	80%
6%	Lack of energy	91	88	97%
17%	Memory loss	265	193	73%
17%	Metallic taste	260	247	95%
7%	Multiple sclerosis	113	86	76%

57 The data represents a partial statistical symptom summary of 1569 patients who participated in six different studies evaluating the health effects of replacing mercury-containing dental fillings with non-mercury substitutes. The data was derived from the following studies: 762 patients' adverse reaction reports submitted to the FDA by the individual patients; 519 patients in Sweden reported on by Mats Hanson Ph.D.; 100 patients in Denmark, treated by Henrik Lichtenberg, D.D.S.; 80 patients in Canada, treated by Pierre Larose, D.D.S.; 86 patients in Colorado, reported on by Robert L. Siblerud, O.D., M.S., as partial fulfilment of a Ph.D. requirement and 22 patients reported on by Alfred V. Zamm, M.D., FACA, FACP.

% of total	Reporting symptom	Cases	Cases improved or cured	% cure/ improved
8%	Muscle tremor	126	104	83%
10%	Nervousness	158	131	83%
8%	Numbness anywhere	118	97	82%
20%	Skin disturbances	310	251	81%
9%	Sore throat	149	128	86%
6%	Tachycardia	97	68	70%
4%	Thyroid problems	56	44	79%
12%	Ulcers/sores in mouth	189	162	86%
7%	Urinary tract problems	115	87	76%
29%	Vision problems	462	289	63%

From this data it can be seen that there was a marked improvement of all the various symptoms upon removal of amalgam.

A woman, 34 years old, came to the clinic complaining of fatigue, dizziness, depression, irritability, bloating and a metal taste in mouth. By using Applied Kinesiology tests she was found to be sensitive to the shigella bacteria, which is always found in cow's milk, and her amalgam filling (she only had one). She was told to avoid cow's milk and to take turmeric and fennel. Nux Vomica 30 was also prescribed.

She returned three months later, having felt better for a while, but then having relapsed. Although using goat's milk, cooking cheese to kill the bacteria and avoiding other dairy foods, she still harboured the shigella bacteria, which was causing problems. Testing showed that the root of the problem was the amalgam filling. She was told that this was her maintaining cause and, until she had it removed, the remedies would just palliate or not work at all. She went to a dentist who removed the filling. Two months later she came back to the clinic and stated that her symptoms had cleared up.

An article in 'Top Sante', March 2005, cited a case where a lady was in so much pain she had to give up her successful job. She started having muscle pains and headaches, then bouts of irritable bowel syndrome, thrush, burning sensations and sinus problems. After two years of this she couldn't function and felt suicidal. From research she found that it could be due to her amalgam fillings. She had 14 fillings, 2 nerve root canal fillings and a crown, so she started to replace them. After a day of each filling removal she felt more energetic and the despair lifted. She had all her fillings out and 2 years on felt 85% better. She stated that "for five years I felt like I had a big wad of cotton wool in my head".

Some people have found that problems following replacement were due to amalgam being left under the substitute. Recent research in Sweden shows that there may be an answer for many of these intractable cases. Dr Christer Malmström has discovered that most of the people who do not see health improvements after amalgam replacement appear to have diverticulum or impacted faecal matter in their colon that contains high levels of toxic metals. Upon removal of these metals e.g. through the process of colonic irrigation, great progress can be seen in the individual's health (Ziff,S. Ziff,M and Hanson,M. Dental Mercury Detox. Aurora Press, Inc (Santa Fe, USA) 2nd edition 1993).

As an example, irritable bowel syndrome is often the result of mercury fillings that are leaking and creating a toxic environment, which attracts the shigella bacteria and causes it to be pathogenic. It has often been said that there was no IBS in the third world until western man moved in with his refined food – closely followed by dentists who packed the teeth of native people with mercury amalgam, and problems then ensued. This is certainly the view of Hulda Clark, reported in her book, 'The Cure for all Diseases', who has researched many cases where fillings have been removed.

Using Applied Kinesiology, we have come to a similar conclusion. There are cases where, with homœopathic or herbal treatment, there was an improvement but never a cure, until the fillings were replaced with white porcelain or plastic. For example, one patient who had been suffering from Crohn's disease and had seen various homœopaths for constitutional treatment, was found to have a significant sensitivity to mercury amalgam. Although she had only two fillings, their removal caused her to report that she considered herself to be cured of the complaint[58].

According to German bacteriologist Guenther Enderlein, certain bacteria are able to take on multiple forms during a single life cycle. When a person is healthy these microbes live in a symbiotic relationship with other cells and play a helpful role in the body's immune system. Any severe deterioration of the body's internal environment however, and they can change into disease-forming agents. Simply put, "The germ is nothing, the terrain is everything": tradititionally this is said to be Louis Pasteur's death-bed quote[59].

Many dentists consider that mercury acts in the mouth somewhat like a battery, in that it holds electrical charges. When the problematical filling is changed, the charge can sometimes jump to another filling, which will then need attention. Everyone has a limited tolerance to mercury. Some people cannot cope with one or two fillings, whereas others can manage with half a mouthful – but the tolerance level decreases as the fillings get older and deteriorate.

58 'Gut Reaction', vol. 7, autumn 1992
59 Mothering, Spring 1994

A couple of cases we have seen in our clinics are a 46-year old male suffering with chronic piles. Upon testing it was found that one of his amalgam fillings was weakening him. He had the filling replaced and his piles were no longer a problem. Another patient, a 38-year-old female, had had a tight, wheezy chest for several months. Upon having her amalgam filling replaced, she vomited that night and the tightness in her chest eased.

In addition to the chemical toxicity of mercury fillings, we have also found that patients with several amalgam fillings generally have an increased sensitivity to electromagnetic stress as well (see Chapter 7).

METALS WHICH WE WEAR AND THOSE IN OUR ENVIRONMENT

We were not designed to wear metal in our teeth or through parts of our bodies. Fillings in our teeth can mean that our tolerance of earrings, necklaces and other items of jewellery is reduced; people will often say that they cannot wear certain metals, especially piercings, because they break out in a rash. What is less well known is that this susceptibility will often lead to the toxicity going inwards and affecting the bloodstream. As the body attempts to protect the vital organs, e.g. the heart and lungs, so toxins are pushed towards the extremities, which can lead to deposits in the joints of the fingers, toes, knees, etc. Rheumatism may develop and this may be more pronounced if the patient is dehydrated as a result of drinking too little water, or too much coffee. If the kidneys are not able to function properly through dehydration, then those deposits in the joints are more likely to stay there causing pain and inflammation.

When treating people and looking for maintaining causes, two questions are generally asked: of the causes we find, which is the most unnatural? And which is the easiest to deal with? Should they be the same, then this is certainly where efforts should be concentrated. An interesting case in point was demonstrated with a horse, which as a foal had succumbed to liver disease. It was now subject to profuse sweating and salivation – unusual symptoms for a horse. It enjoyed clean air and water and the symptoms were no different whether it was grazing on grass in the field or eating hay in the stable. The liver is the organ responsible for the processing of toxins; as it was under-functioning this pointed to an inability to deal with something that had no natural metabolic niche. Because of the increase in saliva, the metal bit in the mouth was prime suspect and, once this was changed to one made of a different substance, the symptoms ceased.

Another case was of a 20-year-old woman who had developed eczema. She came for an appointment saying that her condition had started suddenly six weeks earlier. When asked if there had been any undue stress or anything else happening in her life around that time, she thought and then said, "I had my nipple pierced seven weeks ago". Changing the metal of the piercings to pure gold or silver brought about an immediate improvement in her condition.

A health practitioner began to develop a cough and hayfever symptoms that were getting worse. A week before the problem started she had purchased a cheap, but attractive, pair of earrings that she had worn constantly and, with these removed, the symptoms began to slowly abate. The effect of the metal entering her system was apparently making her much more susceptible to pollen, as well as affecting her chest directly.

In '*The Cure for all Diseases*', Dr Hulda Clark writes,

> *"Biochemists know that a mineral in raw element form always inhibits the enzyme using that mineral. Inorganic copper, like you would get from a copper bottomed kettle or copper plumbing, is carcinogenic".*

Hulda Clark's research led her to conclude that copper pipes could be involved with leukaemia, schizophrenia and fertility problems. Leg cramps are a common result of a sensitivity to copper. Homœopathy is a system of medicine based on the principle of 'like cures like', or 'the hair of the dog that bit you'. Cuprum 30, a homœopathic medicine made from copper, is a number one treatment for leg cramps. We have also seen various benefits when a contraceptive copper IUD (coil) has been removed; these have varied from the cessation of a vaginal discharge to systemic changes not associated with gynaecological function. As the copper is absorbed into the body it can affect other organs, and we have seen both eczema and stomach disorders cured following its removal.

Now obviously we are not saying that copper is responsible for all eczema, or that everyone will experience health benefits when they have their coil removed; we are simply saying that metals are a common form of pollutant, widely found to be behind many conditions. Everyone has a certain susceptibility to them and factors such as our genes, the amount of metal dental fillings, other jewellery, and stress, can decrease our tolerance levels. The problem with much scientific research is that it is trying to find a cure-all for eczema and asthma, but it will never find one because 'John' will have eczema for one reason and 'Janet' for another. In each case the diagnosis and cure must be individual.

In discussing high blood pressure, Dr Hulda Clark found cadmium to blame in most cases. Cadmium is found in galvanised pipes and the elements of electric kettles. Now there are always two ways to work; one way is to 'pull out all the stops', and the other is to take a step at a time. If we were to pull out all the stops, we would have our pipework changed – but, of course, most people have metal pipes but not all of them have high blood pressure. There have to be other factors as well, including our genetic inheritance. Little can be done about genetics, although homœopathic remedies may lessen the effects. Genetic inheritance means that pollutants, such as metals, may cause high blood pressure in one person, but irritable bowel syndrome in someone else.

Now, very often the problem with metals is one of overload. If someone were not wearing certain metals in, on or through their body they would probably find it easier to cope with the problems caused by water pipes.

Gold and silver will generally, by themselves, not cause severe reactions, but often what they are mixed with in jewellery to prevent tarnishing can poison the system. Often we find that a gold earring is fine, but the post that goes through the ear is toxic to the system. Similarly, just the clasp or fastener will have other metals included in it for the hardening effect, and sometimes this in itself is enough to lead to a toxic reaction in the body. This fact led Dr Hulda Clark to write, "Don't wear metal jewellery. Earring posts should be plastic, metal watches and metal-rimmed glasses should be replaced with all plastic types". If you have no way of checking tolerance to individual items of jewellery, this is good general advice.

A 15-year-old girl had been suffering from a sore throat and loss of voice for a week since her baptism. Upon testing she was found to be sensitive to the silver chain, supporting a cross, which she had been given as a present at the baptism and had been wearing ever since. Upon removing the necklace, her throat got better and her voice came back. Another case is of a 34-year-old woman who tried to give blood, but was turned away because she was anaemic. Upon testing, copper came up as a sensitivity. It then turned out that she had an intra-uterine device (coil) which consisted of copper. This seemed to somehow be causing an imbalance with copper in her body; copper is needed to absorb iron, so this seemed to explain her anaemia.

It is very heartening to see the surprise, or even astonishment, of patients who, after removing a necklace or pair of earrings, find that over the next month all their IBS symptoms or migraines clear up. A common comment is, "I never thought removing something so small would make so much difference". Another comment often heard is, "I thought that it was pure gold". This includes comments on gold teeth fillings, which are often mixed with nickel to harden them. It is on these that many bacteria feed, which then cause problems in certain organs. We were meant to live with bacteria, but not to feed them with toxins so that they become pathogenic.

It would be easy to make this book twice the length by discussing metals in the environment. There is cadmium in the elements of electric kettles and pipes which gets into water that can cause raised blood pressure; there is lead in exhaust fumes and some water pipes and in the solder used on food cans. All this contributes to lowering our resistance to other metals. Advice to avoid using metal cutlery other than stainless steel may be sensible, but not always practical. Normally, however, we have found that by avoiding wearing metals as we have described, the body is able to cope much better with the general environmental pollutants. Perhaps, if these environmental pollutants did not exist, we could cope more easily with the jewellery, but the question is, which is easier to deal with, and the answer is obvious. We find that if metals are causing a problem, by dealing with metal items being worn, the patient soon returns to full health – unless an excess of metals from other sources is working to undermine the process.

Here again the use of acupressure techniques described in Appendix 2 can reduce sensitivities to metals.

METALS AS AN AERIAL OR CONDUCTOR

There is a further reason why metals are causing a problem: with the increase in electronic technology, they may be acting as an aerial. In this instance, metals may be a problem if the person is exposed to electromagnetic frequencies such as mobile phones, or working in front of a computer.

If, despite degaussing (see Chapter 7) and using a protector against electromagnetic stress, people are still tired after working on a computer, then it is likely that something they are wearing is attracting electromagnetic fields and severely limiting the beneficial effects of these measures. A problem here is that the metal does not even have to have contact with the skin; it just needs to be very close, and this opens up a whole new field. Zips, buttons, hairgrips, spectacles, clothes fastenings, even bra clips, can sometimes be a problem. Under these circumstances it is necessary either to avoid certain items of clothing for a few days to see if any difference is observed (which may not be immediate), or to find a practitioner who uses kinesiology, or some similar technique, to test for sensitivities.

Dr Hulda Clark's advice to avoid wearing metals is generally good, unless you have excellent health or some way of checking that items do not cause a problem. The number of people who are sensitive to wrist watches has surprised us, but there are normally two reasons for this. It can be that metal alloys are being absorbed through the skin, or it may be related to the battery and hence be electromagnetic stress. We have seen asthma, acne and digestive problems disappear just by consigning the watch to a handbag or briefcase or leaving jewellery at home.

We have also found metal framed spectacles to be a problem, causing the wearer to be even more susceptible to electromagnetic stress. Due to the close proximity of this 'aerial' to the brain, the whole body can be affected. We recommend that people buy solid plastic frames whenever possible.

CHAPTER 10

CANCER IN A CARTON?

So much has been written about smoking, does anything new need to be added? There are many statistics that point to the health dangers.

Back in 1912 lung cancer was called "the rarest of diseases"[60]. In the 1920s it began to increase, and in the '40s and '50s the figures increased at an unbelievable rate and continued to rocket. In 1949, Dr Wynder, in America supplied the first statistical evidence of a link between smoking and lung cancer. He reported that of 605 cases in men, only 8 had been non-smokers. From England came a report that in a study of 1,357 cases of lung cancer, only 7 non-smokers were found.

Cigarettes, as well as containing tar and nicotine, can also legally contain more than 600 additives. These include coffee extract, sugar, vanilla, menthol, cocoa, caramel and chlorophyll. When cocoa burns it produces bromine gas, which causes the air passages to dilate, therefore increasing the amount of nicotine that can be absorbed. Menthol is thought to numb the throat so that smoking is easier. The tobacco companies have specially designed cigarettes so that nicotine can be delivered to its optimum. As well as being addictive, nicotine causes constriction of the blood vessels, which raises blood pressure and puts a strain on the heart[61]. As well as the chemicals in the tobacco being harmful, the filters can also cause harm. They are usually made from cellulose acetate, and studies suggest that some of these fibres end up being inhaled or ingested[62].

There is also more and more research being done into passive smoking and its consequences. A major review

60 Alton Ochsner, 'Smoking and Cancer', New York, Julian Messner, Inc. 1954
61 http://news.bbc.co.uk/1/hi/health/background_briefings/smoking/281167.stm
62 www.btconnect.co.uk/lifework/lifeworknews/topic/TheModernWorld

by the Government-appointed Scientific Committee on Tobacco and Health (SCOTH) concluded that "passive smoking is a cause of lung cancer and ischaemic heart disease in adult non-smokers, and a cause of respiratory disease, cot death, middle ear disease and asthmatic attacks in children". This has led to more and more work places becoming non-smoking. Countries such as southern Ireland and England have now banned smoking from all social areas.

The statistics appear to speak for themselves, until they are put alongside other reports – of Tibetans smoking in the Himalayas and Native Americans in the Appalachian mountains, who live to a ripe old age with never a hint of lung cancer.

Our clinical experience would confirm that generally smoking by itself does not directly cause lung cancer, and we are unaware of any reports linking smoking with the likes of breast or prostate cancer. This statement may fly in the face of much medical thought, but our opinion is that what smoking does is create a toxic area in the lungs and a breakdown of tissue in that area. This can lead directly to conditions such as emphysema, but for cancer there appears to be another active ingredient.

Smoking makes the lungs the body's most vulnerable organ, which means that, with the increase in electronic technology which can lead to cancer, smoking will cause the seat of that cancer to be the lungs. However, about four times as many smokers die of circulatory problems as die of lung cancer, and we do find this to be directly linked to smoking. Also in pulmonary diseases, such as pneumonia, influenza, tuberculosis and asthma, the death rate is nearly three times as high in smokers than with non-smokers[63]. Smoking can also affect the liver, the body's main organ of detoxification, and maintain a state of hepatitis. So smoking is bad for you!

63 E.C. Hammond and Daniel Horn's 'Smoking and Death Rates Report on 44 Months of Follow-Up of 187,783 Men' , 'Journal of the American Medical Association', March 15, 1958, p.1296

When people say "I have lung cancer because I smoked all my life", in a sense they are correct; smoking makes the lungs into toxic organs, which is why they succumbed to lung cancer. If they had been using strong antiperspirants and wearing tight bras restricting the lymph flow, or using certain types of H.R.T., they may have succumbed to breast cancer instead. However, for cancer to develop, generally there has to be another factor, and so this brings us back to geopathic or electromagnetic stress as being the root cause of the problem. From our clinical experience we find that for cancer to develop (in addition to genetics, stress and toxic chemicals playing a role) electromagnetic and/or geopathic stress is also generally present. Therefore if you can remove the electromagnetic and/or geopathic stress, then the chances of developing cancer could be a lot slimmer. This would also help to explain why some smokers develop cancer, whilst others (like many Native Americans) do not. There must be some hidden factor and we think that it is electromagnetic stress and/or geopathic stress.

Kinesiology is not in itself a cure for cancer, but we have seen the prognoses for people with lung cancer, and the results of cancer treatment, improve dramatically after electromagnetic fields have been addressed.

CHAPTER 11

NUTRITION

No book could be written on the maintaining causes of ill health without consideration being given to nutrition. A healthy 'terrain' is dependent on a proper diet, which means foods that are unrefined, organically grown and preservative-free. An improper diet tends to overwhelm the system and leads to disease. Disease symptoms are often a manifestation of the body's efforts to cleanse itself and get rid of excess toxins and waste material. In addition to sound nutrition, a healthy body requires adequate rest and sanitary living conditions. When all these requirements are met, many diseases will pass as sub-clinical infections, without acute illness, or, if there is illness, it will be relatively mild.

Whilst lack of food is rarely the maintaining cause in the western world, a poor diet will lower the immune system and make us less resilient to the other stresses mentioned. Approximately 60% of the population eat 'off the shelf' food, with low fibre and high sugar content. Cookery is rarely taught in school these days. Patients should be given sensible nutritional advice; for example, in the case of rheumatoid arthritis, the more moderate use of tea, coffee, alcohol, sugar and animal products may help. Medicines do not give the body the raw materials; these must come from the diet or healthy supplements. Many patients suffering with chronic cases of disease would benefit from the use of herbal remedies and/or nutritional advice. Hahnemann spoke about syphilis, writing:

"After removing all hurtful influences that affect the patients from without, and after settling on a light yet nourishing and strengthening diet for the patient, let him give the .... medicine"[64]

64 (The Chronic Diseases; Theoretical Part', Samuel Hahnemann.

In an interview in May 2000 Sara Da Silva, a practising homœopath, said that her experience of sending people to nutritionists was often not satisfactory. Her patients did not get enough practical advice about food, but were told to buy vitamins and were put on a restricted diet. That was the reason she started to study nutrition herself – in order to give her patients practical advice about food and nutritional supplements.

Da Silva said that food intolerance is a huge problem nowadays and that she looks at food in the first session with a patient. She said it is fundamental to know what the patients eat and how they eat – are they relaxed, do they eat 'on the run', do they chew their food? The amount of fibre in the diet is, in her opinion, very important.

We can take a relatively healthy child who is producing a lot of mucus. By excluding from his diet wheat and dairy products, which can cause a lot of congestion, we can often see a significant improvement. Another example is a sluggish child who craves carbohydrates. We need to ensure that he drinks enough and has psyllium, linseed or prunes in his diet, as he is very likely to be constipated. Advising that raw salad should be eaten before the main meal to stimulate the digestive system is often enough to cause an improvement in health. Sara Da Silva says that it is very important that doctors and health practitioners know about nutrition – for example, such facts as iron is found in dark green vegetables, and that to absorb it properly, we need vitamin C simultaneously in a natural balanced form.

Although claimed as progress, the process of refining foods has its drawbacks. A clear example of this is demonstrated by research carried out 20 years ago on severe hysteria in dogs, associated with convulsions that ended in death. The results showed that nitrogen trichloride, used as a whitener in flour, altered the chemical composition of the wheat gluten. This flour was used in dog biscuits.

> *"Concern was immediately felt lest the same substance should have some long-term deleterious effect on human beings who consumed white flour, although it was not associated with hysteria of the type encountered in dogs. The use of nitrogen trichloride as a whitening agent in the preparation of flour was abolished by law in the USA and in Britain"* *'Man, Nature & Disease', Richard Fiennes*

It is often said that if we eat a sensible balanced diet, we should have no need for other supplements. There is truth in this. In the past there was no need for vitamin supplements, but today how do we obtain that ideal diet? In 1936 a report to the American Senate said that due to intensive agriculture and lack of crop rotation the average American diet was not sufficient for health and well-being. If that was the case in 1936, how much more is it true today with intensive farming, the demineralisation of soil and the artificial fertilisers and preservatives that get into our food. The World Health Organisation says that supplementation is now necessary; an estimated 84% of nutrients are not absorbed by the body due to processing, chemicals and additives. They may get into the bloodstream, but not to the cells that need them. For our ancestors this used to be only 7% – health foods used to be called 'groceries'!

There is a well-known phrase, "you are what you eat". Perhaps a better version would be "you are what you assimilate". A walk around the supermarket will show many foods to be calcium-enriched or fortified with iron, but much of this is in a form that the body cannot use. Reports showed that a legal requirement to put calcium into bread was useless because the body could not assimilate it. And the cooking of food can destroy many vitamins and enzymes. Whilst the making of bread will destroy some of the vitamin B content, a slice of toast will have only about 30% of the vitamin B content of the same amount of bread when untoasted.

Whilst few diseases today in the western world are directly caused by malnutrition, a lack of essential nutrients will lower the immune system and the body's resilience. This makes us more susceptible both to acute disease and to other environmental pollutants such as metals, electromagnetic stress and normal stress which our liver would otherwise be able to deal with suitably.

SUPPLEMENTS

This brings us to the need for supplementation. In both chemists and health food shops we are met by a dazzling array of supplements, and the question arises of which ones should we use. Added to this, research has shown many vitamin and mineral supplements to be useless and some to be even harmful in large and continued doses. This has led to legislation banning some supplements in certain countries. From clinical experience we have to agree with this. When vitamins are synthesised and taken away from their natural food state they become drugs in their own right, and all drugs taken for a long period can produce side effects.

In 1911 a Polish chemist, Casimir Funk, first coined the name 'vitamin' when working on a cure for beri-beri, and since that time scientists have been researching the components of food. Vitamin C was officially recognised in 1928 and was first produced chemically in 1933, when its structural formula was established. Apart from iron, calcium and iodine, little attention was paid to minerals until much later, so we are dealing with a very new science. Because of this it is very difficult for scientists to get the balance right. The effect of taking synthetically-produced vitamins in isolation from their natural carrier in food is largely unknown, but tests done on patients in our London clinic show that many of these have a negative impact. In fact they deplete the body of certain trace elements in order to use the ones in the vitamin pills. It is common for patients to arrive with a carrier bag full of vitamin C, selenium, zinc, iron, etc. and be more concerned about whether they should be taking something else as well, rather than whether they are taking the correct balance.

We know that 1gm of vitamin C daily can put a strain on the kidneys and cause silt, gravel or stones, even though it is generally considered safe and water-soluble. The kidneys were not designed to eliminate so much ascorbic acid (vitamin C), and what they cannot handle they will put a protective coating around (i.e. silt and gravel). Diarrhoea, gout and infertility have also been linked to taking excessive vitamin C daily for several months. Similarly excess vitamin A over a period of time can result in an enlarged spleen and liver, painful swelling under the skin, stunted bone growth, skull pressure and an increased risk of skin cancer. Too much vitamin B can cause an irregular heartbeat and stomach problems[65].

So we are left with a nutritional shortfall in much of our food and many supplements costing a lot of money, but of dubious benefit. Indeed, some of those most widely advertised seem to be the worst. None of the previously mentioned side effects have been found when the supplement is in a completely balanced state, so therefore we need a supplement in a totally balanced form, and which is nearly 100% absorbable.

Whilst we are not saying that there is only one answer to this conundrum, over the years of testing we have found algae from Lake Klamath to be one of the best vitamin/mineral supplements on the market (see Appendix 8). It grows in a lake in southern Oregon, which is fed by 17 mineral-rich streams and geothermal springs – vitamins need minerals for their production. Algae, being the most primitive plant form, have a semi-permeable cell membrane and therefore 96 percent of the nutritional

65 'Vitamins, what they are and why we need them', Carol Hunter, Thorsons, 1978

content can be assimilated by the cells that need it. In this way we have not a 'magic medicine', but simply a supplement that will deal with the nutritional aspect of most problems.

My personal and first encounter with Lake Klamath algae was when the offices of Aquasource, an algae supplier, moved into one of the colleges where I was lecturing. Many of the students were taking it and said that they had more energy. A number of the women acknowledged a reduction in pre-menstrual tension as the algae helped to balance the blood sugar levels. When I spoke to a herbalist based at our London clinic about this subject, he commented that whilst many herbal remedies were supposed to increase the patient's energy, the only thing that he had ever prescribed which really did have this effect in patients was Lake Klamath algae. This is rarely the case when using algae that is freeze-dried, as this process can destroy valuable enzymes. Therefore it really is essential to use a brand that is either vacuum or low-temperature air-dried.

The personal experience of one of the authors was not that of a sudden burst of energy, but simply a reduction in catching colds. Being a health practitioner is a little like being a school teacher, in that one is constantly assailed by germs. Teachers and health practitioners often complain of constant colds (an embarrassing side effect of their jobs), but the authors have found that, since taking a few algae capsules each day, they catch very few colds from patients, and if they do succumb, they recover much more quickly than would otherwise be the case.

Perhaps the two most common mineral deficiencies are of iron and calcium. Lake Klamath algae contains over 34mg of absorbable iron in every gram and this helps to boost energy levels. A pregnant woman had been diagnosed as anaemic and was constantly feeling tired. She was reluctant to take chemical iron tablets because they had made little difference to her sense of wellbeing in previous pregnancies and had caused constipation. On just two algae capsules a day she began to feel more like her old self and hospital tests showed a significant rise in her haemoglobin levels.

Similarly each gram of algae contains about 28mg of absorbable calcium. Osteoporosis appears to be on the increase despite, or possibly because of, the modern diet, and two patients on the borders of the disease readily spring to mind. They showed significant improvements in bone density after having taken the algae for a few months. Not long ago we met a former patient, a well-known jazz band leader, in a local restaurant. We shared with him that we were about to lecture on the subject of algae. He commented that he continued to take it and said, "Tell them that my nails have been growing much stronger and quicker since taking it. I have to cut them much more often now!" The algae had obviously been nourishing his nails, which are rich in calcium and silica. A similar story from patients is that hair is thicker, stronger and in better condition.

But, perhaps the most commonly heard story from patients is that of a general feeling of wellbeing. Sometimes this is recognised more by people if they stop taking the algae for a while; they then realise how much better they had been feeling. To repeat, it is not a 'magic medicine'; it is just dealing generally with the nutritional side of people's problems (we should emphasise again that freeze-dried brands rarely produce the same comments).

A while ago I received an unsolicited letter saying,

"Just a note to say that I am very pleased with the algae you sent me. For a long time I've suffered with indigestion and excessive gas despite a vegetarian diet. Within a day or two of taking the algae things improved. After a week the bloated feeling has almost gone, my sleep has improved and I feel much better".

A fellow practitioner wrote to me saying that in the previous two years she had probably put between 75 and 100 patients on algae. The main improvements people reported were increased stamina and energy, and a greater ability to cope with tiredness. A couple of women with ulcerative colitis felt it helped their bowel function. Some people felt it helped them to pass a good stool in the morning. A woman with severe pre-menstrual fluid retention found that, as soon as she had an algae capsule in each morning, she passed large quantities of urine and her ankle oedema was much reduced. A female with a tendency to recurrent cystitis now regularly increases her algae intake by 3-4 capsules daily if she feels the onset of any urinary discomfort; needless to say, she has tubs of algae all over the house, and in her car, in her bag etc! A female with Bell's palsy/Ramsay Hunt syndrome did very well on homœopathic medication, but as her pain reduced she had a return of sinusitis. She increased her algae intake to 6 capsules for two days and felt a marked improvement. In the practitioner's own case, her stamina is much improved and her haemoglobin level increased from 8.5g/dl to 10.5 in a few months.

In using nutrition and algae we are not working to destroy, kill or cure a disease, but rather to create a healthy person who is less susceptible to the organisms and pollutants that affect so much of the population.

MILK

The following appeared in 'The Metro' July 14th 2003:

> *"Deadly toll as fatty foods peril ignored. Heart and cancer deaths are set to soar after a survey found Britons ignoring fatty food warnings. Saturated fats should not contribute more than 11 percent to an adult's daily energy intake. But a Government study showed the average for men was 13.4 percent and women 13.2 percent. Milk and cheese were the main culprits, followed by meat, burgers, pizza, bread, biscuits and cakes".*

Whilst other factors are involved, low quality nutrition will make us more susceptible to these complaints.

We cannot avoid further reference to dairy products. There is a general consensus of opinion that milk is good for us and, if we do not drink cow's milk, then we will be lacking in calcium. Nature, however, designed cow's milk for calves not humans. Non-boiled (including pasteurised) milk contains the shigella bacteria, and many babies who come to the clinic are found to have a problem with this. Dill and fennel are ingredients in many types of gripe water both because they are antispasmodic and also because they help with the intestinal flora, assisting the stomach to mature so that it can cope with the intake of shigella. Many people who travel to the East, but continue with a British-style diet, may succumb to shigella, e-coli, giardia and other organisms. The local people may not suffer these problems because their national diet, containing spices such as turmeric and cinnamon, helps to cleanse the gut. Hence herbalists widely use turmeric and fennel to normalise the environment of the intestine.

Not only colic, but also catarrh, mucus and congestion are very common in people who are given cow's milk too young in life, before their systems have the maturity to cope with it. Research has also linked cow's milk to obesity, heart disease, diabetes, asthma and even osteoporosis. The following is edited from the Internet home page of Robert "Notmilkman" Cohen: www.notmilk.com:

> *"A study at the University of Helsinki*[66] *revealed that early introduction of cow's milk in babies three months of age or younger often resulted in complete insulin deficiency. This pathology occurred because naturally occurring beta cells were destroyed by the infant's allergic reaction created in response to the presence of cow's milk proteins".*

66 Virtanen and Aro, 'Dietary factors in the aetiology of diabetes', Ann. Med. 26 (6): 469-478, Dec. 1994

Scientists in Italy noted similar effects after analysing data from diabetic children. Their conclusion indicated an absolute cause and effect relationship between milk consumption and diabetes[67].

There will be other key factors present, discussed elsewhere in this book which, when present, make people more sensitive to dietary factors.

An article in the 'New York Times' on May 5th 1999 read that 38% of homeless children have asthma. There was a photo of a small Afro-American boy wearing an oxygen mask and the comment that they get free cheese and milk, which serve as the foundation of their diet.

80% of milk protein is casein, used as glue to hold wood together in furniture. Eat casein and you produce histamines, which result in mucus, which makes breathing difficult. Asthma results when the bronchioles of the lungs fill with sticky mucus. We have found that with true asthma there is also a problem with the organism ascaris. Behind these cases we generally find that geopathic stress, electromagnetic stress, metals or dehydration is a problem – or sometimes cat dander or saliva. More research needs to be done on whether milk makes one more susceptible to the above, or whether sometimes the above makes one more susceptible to a reaction to milk.

It may seem surprising to link osteoporosis to the consumption of milk, yet the facts speak for themselves. To again refer to Robert "Notmilkman" Cohen's website, we find the following:

"American women have been consuming an average of two pints of milk per day for their entire lives, yet thirty million American women have osteoporosis. Drinking milk does not prevent bone loss. Bone loss is accelerated by ingesting

67 Fava et al., 'Relationship between dairy product consumption and the incidence of IDDM in childhood in Italy', Diabetes Care 17 (12): 1488-90, Dec. 1994

> *too much protein, and milk has been called 'liquid meat'. Osteoporosis is a big health issue".*

About 50,000 Americans die each year of problems related in some way to osteoporosis[68]. This links into the research that Osteoporosis is caused by a number of things, one of the most important being too much dietary protein[69]. In the US the average man eats 175% more protein than the recommended daily allowance and the average woman eats 144% more[70]. Surprisingly, drinking more milk to reduce your risks of osteoporosis actually can have the opposite affect and cause more of a problem. This is partly because in order to absorb calcium, the body needs comparable amounts of another mineral element, magnesium. Milk and dairy products contain only small amounts of magnesium. Magnesium is the central element in the chlorophyll molecule, therefore intake of green vegetation is essential if the calcium is to be properly utilised.

> *"Countries with the highest rates of osteoporosis, such as the United States, England and Sweden, consume the most milk. China and Japan, where people eat much less dairy food, have low rates of osteoporosis"*
>
> *'Nutrition Action Healthletter', June 1993*

More about possible links between milk and other diseases, from rheumatism to kidney stones, heart disease, obesity, bowel problems and allergies can be found on the previously mentioned website, www.notmilk.com.

We will just mention in passing the distressing condition of acne. Milk can be part of the problem, as there can be unnatural hormones present in the milk which the body then has to try and eliminate. However, it can get to a point where the body can no longer cope. A milk-free diet for a period could do much to alleviate the condition.

A teenager came to the clinic with acne. Testing showed a sensitivity to milk and upon questioning it

68 'Osteoporosis International' 1993, 3, (3)
69 'Science' 1986, 233 (4763)
70 Surgeon General's Report on Nutrition and Health, 1988

was discovered that he drank over a pint every day. He reduced his milk intake and this led to clearer skin.

Another woman found that milk played a significant role in the flare-ups of her eczema. This was not the case if she drank organic milk.

CANDIDA

We have never found it necessary to use a direct germ-killing regime against candida and other fungi. More efficient is changing the internal environment, which then reduces the threat of the organism, causing it to have a benign action in the body. There is much interest in candida and we find many patients consider that candida is their main problem. However, we find that candida is significant in only about 10% of patients, and treatment for this would be the same as for any other organism. It would mean finding the relevant pollutant as described in this book which will create an environment in which the candida can thrive and cause problems. The reason will vary from individual to individual.

MICROWAVING FOOD

In today's society, modern technology has provided us with a very quick way of heating up our food and most kitchens in the Western world have a microwave oven in them. Over 90% of American homes have microwave ovens used for meal preparation[71]. However, more and more research is finding that microwaved food, rather than nourishing us, may actually be detrimental to our health.

Microwave ovens work by bombarding the food with microwaves which in turn causes the water molecules within the food to vibrate, creating friction which generates heat and warms up the food. However these vibrations also cause damage to the surrounding molecules, deforming them:

71 www.choosecra.com/htmlpages/news/reports/mocrowavedanger.html

> *"A basic hypothesis of natural medicine states that the introduction into the human body of molecules and energies to which it is not accustomed is much more likely to cause harm than good. Microwaved food contains both molecules and energies not present in food cooked in the way humans have been cooking food since the discovery of fire. Artificially produced microwaves are produced from alternating current and force a billion or more polarity reversals per second in every food molecule they hit. Production of unnatural molecules is inevitable. Naturally occurring amino acids have been observed to undergo isomeric changes as well as transformation into toxic forms, under the impact of microwaves in ovens."*[72]

There was a lawsuit in 1991 in Oklahoma after a woman who had hip surgery was killed by a simple blood transfusion when a nurse "warmed the blood for the transfusion in a microwave oven"! Blood for transfusion is routinely warmed but not in a microwave oven. Is this because the blood is subtly altered during the microwaving process?

We have also found in our own experimentation that whilst blue-green algae is a very good nutritional support, after microwaving it offers nothing! We therefore need to give more thought to how we prepare our food. Instead of opting for the quick, convenient microwave we should use the oven or hob instead, thus reducing the loss of valuable nutrients within our food.

72 'Scientific Evidence and Facts In a Comparative Study of Food Prepared Conventionally and in the Microwave Oven', published by Raum & Zelt in 1992, at 3 (2):43

CHAPTER 12

WHAT WE PUT ON OUR SKIN

A little now needs to be said about the chemicals which we intentionally or unintentionally put on our bodies.

WASHING POWDERS

One of the major problem-causing substances here is washing powder. When we see patients with a rash around the areas that clothes, especially tight fitting underclothes, are rubbing on, then washing powder is the first thing we consider. This is often the case with babies displaying signs of eczema, whose sensitive skin has not developed sufficiently to be able to withstand some of the harsh chemicals added to the powder to make clothes "whiter than white" or "brighter than bright".

Often some of the major brand names "designed for sensitive skin" are no better. Washing powders and liquids sold by health food shops, or the cheaper 'own brands' of the larger supermarkets generally affect people less, but there is no guarantee. Also, if the powder form is suitable, it is a pointer, but no guarantee, that the tablet form or liquid of the same brand are compatible. Even if the patient has not changed his washing powder, there is always the possibility that the manufacturer has updated it with the addition of more toxic chemicals.

We have often seen eczema, psoriasis, and many so-called 'intractable skin diseases' clear up just by changing the washing powder, often to the amazement of the sufferer, who could not believe that such a small alteration could make so much difference. It may be that a few months after the condition has healed, the skin is sufficiently recovered to once again be able to withstand the abrasive, or chemical, nature of the ingredients. However, in the short term, they should be avoided.

This can be an almost impossible task when sharing a communal machine, such as in a hall of residence or nurses' home. It may take up to four washes to remove all traces of the old powder from the machine and also a couple to get it out of clothes. Therefore every member of the family needs to change. We have seen people who said that their children's eczema had not improved although they had been washing their clothes separately. However they were still using the original substances for their own clothes in the same washing machine; when everything was changed, the condition cleared up. For a child with eczema around its mouth, exacerbated by dribbling, the washing powder used for the pillowcase could be of major importance.

True eczema (as opposed to dermatitis), like psoriasis and asthma, generally involves the organism ascaris. Hulda Clark has repeatedly discussed this in her writings and we are continually verifying it in our clinical experience. Because ascaris is found in dust and animal hair, with which we are all in contact to some degree, the question again is not how do we eliminate the micro-organism, but how do we become less susceptible to its proliferation? Changing washing powder is not a cure-all for eczema: it is a cure for some people's eczema. It is less likely to be relevant if the person also suffers from the related condition of asthma. Powder on clothes will not affect the chest of many people, so here we are more likely to be concerned with some of the other subjects discussed, such as metals, electricity or dehydration.

The cry of many health practitioners in different fields is that eczema and psoriasis are very difficult to treat and often the results are indifferent. Our experience is that psoriasis is usually more stubborn, but many hitherto intransigent cases of eczema have been resolved very quickly using the strategies we are discussing. Psoriasis will progress in a similar way, but it seems that, if there is any area of toxicity, the psoriasis will cling to it. We are therefore working much more to peel off the layers, one at a time, in order to achieve the results.

Whilst washing powders are perhaps the major concern, we should not ignore soaps, bacterial hand washes, hair dyes, shampoos and sun creams. A skin rash confined to the hands may point to soaps, hand wash solutions or chemicals at work. It may be that a person has used the same hand wash for many years but, after a graze or infection, the skin becomes sensitive to what previously may have been completely innocuous.

A patient came who was allergic to cabbages and oranges. She was found to be sensitive to her shampoo and washing powder. Once these were addressed she was no longer sensitive to the oranges and cabbages. This makes you wonder about the massive increase in food allergies over the last decade. How many of these are due to another seemingly unrelated factor?

SUNSCREEN AND SHAMPOO

Hair dyes and shampoos may give rise to skin eruptions and sometimes headaches, but anything absorbed through the skin is likely to affect the more constitutionally weak areas. It could even be responsible for such conditions as colitis, if this is an area of inherited weakness. For instance, Neways, a company providing many plant-based cosmetics, comment on the link between sodium lauryl sulphate, used in many shampoos, and cataracts. A person may be able to tolerate a shampoo on its own, but not the shampoo and conditioner together. This is something that we frequently find.

For a condition such as asthma or colitis the maintaining cause is most often metals, electromagnetic and geopathic stress or dehydration. It is only when removal of these common factors fails to produce the expected results that other options such as exposure to toiletries need to be considered.

There is currently a lot of publicity to use sunscreens to protect ourselves from harmful UV radiation. There was a newspaper article about chemicals in many sun creams contaminating breast milk, but no-one seemed to be asking the question about what else it did when absorbed through the skin. About 90% of sunscreens contain octyl methoxycinnamate (OMC) which was found, by Norwegian scientists, to kill mouse cells even at low doses[73]. This is a concern as in the 1970's Professor Howard Maibad warned that 35% of the sunscreen applied to the skin can pass through the skin into the bloodstream. Another chemical found in sunscreens is oxybenzone, which is an excellent broad spectrum UVA filter. However, it rapidly oxidises when exposed and produces products that could have damaging or harmful effects, as it produces free radicals which are damaging to skin cells and particularly the DNA, which can lead to skin cancer.

The best form of sunscreen is to change your schedule or use a physical barrier, such as a hat, rather than a chemical barrier.

DEODORANTS AND ANTI-PERSPIRANTS

Another concern is deodorants and anti-perspirants. The TV advertisements delight in discussing how certain products will keep you completely dry and how this will help you to attract members of the opposite sex. No one seems to consider that Nature intended us to perspire to eradicate certain toxins. An allergy to chemicals in some deodorants can cause soreness and skin rashes, but the fact that chemicals are being absorbed through the skin and that the body is unable to eliminate toxins can cause more serious problems.

In virtually every case we see of people with cancer there is a problem with electromagnetic or geopathic stress. It is no coincidence that the incidence of cancer has

73 www.mercola.com/2000/oct/15/sunscreen.htm

risen along with the increased use of mobile phones and computers. Once this maintaining cause is removed, the chances of recovery are significantly increased. However the body needs to be able to eliminate its toxic load, and reducing the use of certain anti-perspirants and tight bras, which restrict the lymph flow, can make a significant difference here. An article in the 'Sunday Times' stated:

> *"A possible link between increasing use of anti-perspirants and rising rates of breast cancer is being investigated by scientists. Links have been discovered between some of the ingredients found in common anti-perspirants and the development of tumours. The scientists are now demanding more money for research into chemicals that may be to blame. New cases of breast cancer have doubled from about 20,000 a year in the late 1970s to almost 40,000 a year now. Britain has one of the world's highest rates of the disease and every year almost 13,000 British women die from it. Per head, Britons are also among the biggest users of anti-perspirants."*[74]

Philippa Darbre, a senior cancer researcher in the department of cell and molecular biology at Reading University published in 2004 a comprehensive review of research on the issue. Her conclusions point to a connection between 'underarm cosmetics' and breast cancer.

"The nature of the chemicals in these cosmetics and the lack of any advice about safe quantity or frequency of application should be of concern... The option to be able to do something to reduce the risk of breast cancer has long been awaited and would be welcomed by many women", says Darbre's report.

The formation of malignant breast tumours is known to be linked to hormone levels. Laboratory experiments have indicated that chemical compounds in anti-perspirants derived from zirconium and aluminium may be linked to hormone disruption. These chemicals, absorbed through the skin, can have damaging effects on DNA.

74 Rogers,L. Sunday Times. Sunday 15th June 2003

Researchers say more work needs to be done on whether the small quantities of the chemicals found in anti-perspirants may be dangerous, and how the compounds may affect cancer.

Anti-perspirants were introduced at the beginning of the 20th century. Since then, their use has spiralled with increasing emphasis on personal hygiene and heavy advertising of products aimed at both men and women. Britons are now spending huge amounts on them. Many leading brands contain aluminium-based and/or zirconium-based compounds.

Darbre, whose review is published in the *'Journal of Applied Toxicology'*, pointed out that the rise of breast cancer in men parallels the increase in women and has also doubled over the past three decades to about 300 cases a year.

Most cases of breast cancer occur in the upper outer section of the left breast, the proportion in that area having increased from 31% in 1926 to 61% in 1994.

If anti-perspirants are to blame, this would be accounted for by the fact that use of them has increased and most people are right-handed and likely to apply more anti-perspirant to their left armpit, Darbre said:

> *"There will undoubtedly be individual differences in levels of absorption or toxicity in different people, but more research is urgently needed and at the moment there is little impetus ... There are no instructions about amounts to be applied or frequency of use and the trend for uncontrolled usage of these chemicals well before puberty should be a cause of concern."*

A European Commission report set out a programme of work to investigate how chemicals disrupt human hormones. "We know increased instances of breast cancer have been observed in the West and in countries adopting a western lifestyle", a spokesman said. Generally, body sprays and simple deodorants that are not also anti-perspirants will not contain aluminium or zirconium: but check the ingredients on the label.

Researchers at Reading University found traces of the chemicals called parabens in tumours of breast cancer sufferers. They have proved that these chemical preservatives used in deodorants can accumulate inside the body; however there is yet no proof of a direct link with breast cancer. Dr Philip Harvey, European editor of the 'Journal of Applied Toxicology', stressed:

"further work is required to examine any association between oestrogenic, and other, chemicals in the underarm cosmetics, and breast cancer"[75].

TOOTHPASTE AND MOUTHWASHES

Now let us move on to mention mouth ulcers and gum decay. A patient recently came to our clinic with about 20 mouth ulcers and said that she had been suffering from this complaint for many years. A doctor had suggested that she might have an allergy to her amalgam fillings and suggested that she had them changed. Now, while this could well have been a problem, in her case it may have made no difference at all. We simply advised her to change her toothpaste and, over the following two weeks, all the ulcers disappeared and she has had no recurrence of the problem. Some toothpastes, even those bought from health food shops, can be too abrasive or contain harsh chemicals, especially sodium lauryl/laureth sulphate. Occasionally mouthwashes can have an equally bad effect. An article in the 'Daily Telegraph' read:

"Why your toothpaste could give you ulcers. Toothpaste and mouthwash could be seriously harming our health, according to new research. They can contain detergents which are found in washing-up liquid and washing powder. According to dental experts, these can cause mouth ulcers and seriously damage the surface of teeth. Metals added to toothpaste to make it abrasive – to help whiten teeth – can erode the outer coating of teeth, exposing the softer dentine."

75 www.agora-inc.com/forums

Just as disturbing, separate investigations link alcohol in mouthwashes with oral cancer. The cancer risk to smokers who use alcohol-based washes is increased by 90%. It seems to be the combination of smoking and use of alcohol-based mouth washes that increases the risk so greatly. The British Dental Association has been pressing for reduction in alcohol levels in mouthwashes.

Dentists involved in Scandinavian research are astounded that detergents such as sodium lauryl sulphate and metals are commonly included in toothpastes when there is clear evidence that they cause harm.

Dr Bente Herlofson, of Oslo University Dental School, tried detergent-based toothpaste for three months on patients prone to mouth ulcers. Then she gave them detergent-free toothpaste for three months. At the end of the trial she discovered there had been a 70 percent reduction in mouth ulcers while the patients were on detergent-free toothpaste.

Sodium lauryl sulphate (SLS) is a common ingredient in shampoo, cosmetics and washing powder. It is also widely used as a model detergent for irritant-testing on the skin.

"It can cause skin inflammation and it is not surprising it can damage the soft tissue of the mouth, causing ulcers" says Dr Herlofson.

Most toothpaste on sale in Britain contains up to 3% SLS and few dentists have spoken out against its use. Public relations consultant Nula Bealby had suffered from mouth ulcers most of her life. Her dentist persuaded her to stop using toothpastes containing SLS. As she is a smoker he also advised her to switch to an alcohol-free mouthwash to reduce the risk of cancer. She says:

> *"Until I stopped using detergent-based toothpaste I would get ulcers at least a couple of times a month … I started using detergent-free toothpaste six months ago and I haven't had an ulcer since. My children also had problems, but they haven't had any ulcers since we switched toothpaste".*

FRAGRANCES AND HAIR DYES

> *"Air fresheners and aerosols may have a possible link to stomach upsets and earache in young children say researchers at Bristol University"*
>
> *'The Observer', October 24th 2004*

We have found patients can often be sensitive to fragrances, frequently the perfumes that they use regularly. A 37-year-old female's IBS symptoms cleared up after she stopped using the perfume that she was found to be sensitive to.

People are slowly becoming aware that maybe fragrances have an impact on our health. The *Metro* headlines stated 'Perfumes linked to infertility'. In this article Professor Richard Sharpe said that 'women should stop using body creams and perfumes'.[76]

A woman came to the clinic who had suffered for years from migraines and had seen several other complementary therapists, with no success. Upon testing she was found to go weak on henna and when questioned said that she had been dying her hair for years. A sample of her hair was tested and it came up as a maintaining cause. She stopped dying her hair and her migraines stopped.

We also had another case of someone suffering from teeth problems and an itchy roof of mouth, which cleared up after they stopped dying their hair.

76 Harrison,K. Metro. September 1st 2008

CHAPTER 13

ACUTE DISEASE

Much of our discussion has centred on chronic disease, as acute disease, by definition, is not maintained but is resolved. We are however more likely to become susceptible to a virus or bacteria due to an impaired immune system. If we get a chill or shock, are stressed and/or our diet suffers, then we may succumb to a virus or bacteria.

Now, many of these bacteria and viruses aren't from outside of us, but are living benignly inside our bodies, and all is kept in a natural balance by a healthy immune system (if our bodies are buried after death, the organisms that consume us do not come from outside the coffin!).

It is well known that the measles virus causes measles and the polio virus causes polio, but only if the conditions are right for these diseases to develop. This is confirmed by our research using virus tests (available from www.traditionalhealth.com) and kinesiological muscle response (see Appendix 2). In many cases these viruses will manifest as the common symptoms of a cold or cough, but the full blown symptoms of the disease will not always develop. In the same way it is well known that the streptococcus bacteria can often cause throat infections, but in some people it can cause rheumatism, in others kidney infections. In many people streptococcus can be identified at any time by a throat swab and it coexists with us without problem or difficulty. Using acupressure 'tapping' techniques[77] to stimulate the thymus gland it is possible to desensitise the body to these viruses, and, if there is no maintaining cause, to rapidly return to a state of good health. However, if the immune system is low and the body is in a toxic state then a new virus may take over and cause effects.

77 see Chapter 4, Appendix 2 and '*Health Kinesiology*', Jane Thurnell-Read

Whilst this is only the beginning of new research into the nature of acute disease, it points to the necessity of a healthy diet and the importance of a healthy immune system in order that the many viruses, bacteria and fungi (such as candida) we are in contact with remain benign.

With acute cases we generally find that there is some bacteria, virus, fungi or parasite that is causing the problem. We can desensitise the patient to the pathogen using techniques described in Chapter 4. However, quite often there is some reason why the microbe has become a problem and this can be due to any of the things that have been mentioned throughout this book.

A mother had been suffering from a cough for 2 months and had taken 3 courses of antibiotics. She was seen every day at the clinic for a week, during which time different viruses and bacteria were found due to her lungs being filled with phlegm, providing a very toxic environment for these microbes to occupy. She was desensitised to each one in turn and by the end of the week she was 95% better.

A 23-year-old man presented with mouth ulcers, which he had suffered with for the previous 8 months. He had seen specialists but to no avail. He had had the ulcers since suffering from flu and was sitting in the consultation chewing gum, which he had been doing a lot since giving up smoking. Upon testing he went weak on the influenza virus and the chewing gum. He was then desensitised to both of these and advised to stop chewing the gum or to be tested on another brand. In addition he was prescribed a homœopathic remedy. He reported back that his ulcers had improved dramatically by the next day after these steps were taken.

A 32-year-old female who suffered monthly from cold sores, was treated for the herpes simplex virus. The following month she got the familiar tingling sensation on her lip, but the cold sore didn't erupt. Since then she has suffered from far fewer cold sores, and they are smaller and of shorter duration than those previously suffered. Other environmental factors such as electromagnetic stress need to be addressed in order to further reduce these breakouts.

In some cases of hayfever we get tremendous results from just desensitising the patients to the indicated pollens and grasses. However, in some cases the body will not allow the acupressure tapping to proceed, due to another underlying factor. In these cases, we have often found that it is metals or electromagnetic stress which are actually the problem, and once these have been addressed the pollen is no longer an issue.

In some cases of acute illness, we gather a sample of the person's saliva (which may contain any microbes that they are currently susceptible to) into a little plastic bag, test it, and if required desensitise them to these microbes. This has brought about very quick recoveries and does not require the practitioner to have the test kits to hand. We have also found it useful to give patients suffering from bacterial problems a dose of ozone. The ozone helps to destroy the bacteria and thus speeds up the recovery time.

Antibiotics will annihilate a wide range of bacteria. Acupressure tapping and tolerance tapping will deal with only the bacterium that is causing the problem at the time of testing. Sometimes it is necessary to see someone daily for a few days to clear up the case. A woman aged 86 had had a persistent cough for 3 months and had been on two courses of antibiotics. She was seen 5 days in succession during which she had to be desensitised to two viruses and one bacteria. These procedures eradicated the cough.

Patients seen for acute diseases can be treated using acupressure tapping. However, these patients can often be susceptible to more conditions unless the maintaining cause is addressed, such as smoking, having amalgam fillings, electromagnetic stress or dehydration.

CHAPTER 14

IN CONCLUSION

Our level of health is a reflection of how our body, mind and spirit are responding to our environment and lifestyle. It depends on the air we breathe, the liquid we drink and the food we eat; on the efficiency of the liver, kidneys, skin and other organs of elimination; on our emotions or thought processes and our inherited constitution – all of these play a part.

More important than killing a germ or a disease is to create a healthy person. This requires the establishment of a proper living environment, so that the body can heal itself, and may involve dealing with electromagnetic stress, geopathic stress, metals and dehydration.

Not infrequently, however, a patient may say, "You consider that I have a problem with metals and my earrings, but I am sure that stress is the real cause of the problem". In many ways they are indeed correct, because stress lowers the immune system and makes people more sensitive to the other factors mentioned. We have always (and always will) lived in a stressful world and our bodies were designed to cope with a certain amount of stress.

People in different countries will have different stressful situations; those in developing countries will encounter stress in their quest for food and clean drinking water. Others, in war zones primarily, require protection from their enemies, whereas those of us in the Western world will generally be more susceptible to financial and work-related worries. However, stress exists and, whilst there are ways to minimise its effect, it will always be with us.

The following diagram shows symptoms surrounded by a ring of ill health and we need to break the circle completely in order to get results.

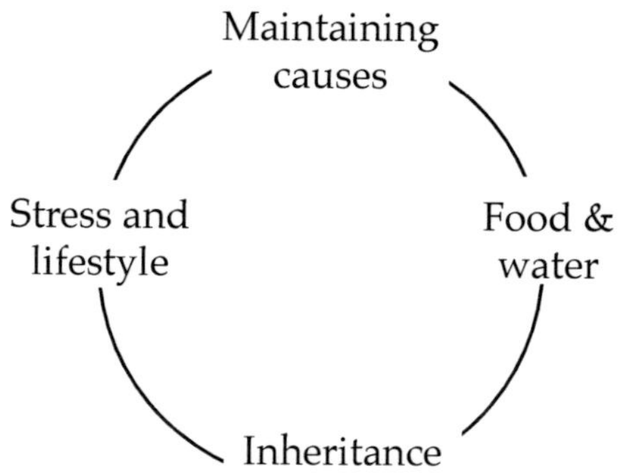

Our inheritance is something that obviously cannot be changed, and it is this factor which affects the way we individually react when we succumb to the aforementioned pollutants: some will get migraines, others stomach disorders, and yet others, breathing problems. Some therapeutic means, such as using constitutional and miasmatic homœopathic remedies, can lessen the sensitivity, in order to reduce the chance or the degree to which we succumb. Nothing however can totally break the circle at this point.

So now let us consider the stress and lifestyle part of the circle. If we can effectively deal with stress, then our internal environment can totally change. For instance, adrenalin is created to enable us to handle stressful situations. Its release can lead to such things as increased blood flow, increased concentration, dilation of the pupils and other functions necessary to perform under stress. After the stress has passed, the adrenalin should be broken down by another hormone, nor-adrenaline. A constant level of stress will just lead to more and more adrenalin being created, a failure in it being broken down properly, and a toxic environment created as a result. In this toxic environment micro-organisms become pathogenic and symptoms appear.

Now, there are various ways of dealing with stress, ranging from meditation and prayer, to aromatherapy and massage, herbal and homœopathic medicine, Bach and other flower remedies, and even chemical drugs (which will not cure the problem, but may help to alleviate symptoms while the person is recovering).

Another method that can work immediately is known as Emotional Stress Release. A useful English idiom is the phrase 'up tight', as it so well describes what happens to us under stress. We get overwhelmed, feel unable to cope, and the thinking part of the brain becomes stressed and paralysed. There is a tightness and spasm, which affects many organs in the body. As the nervous system goes into spasm, there is a 'shutting down', affecting the thinking processes and the flow of blood, gastric juices and hormones.

A practitioner noticed that when people were emotionally distressed and faced with difficult stressful situations, they would often put their hands to their foreheads. He noticed that when people were very upset, they would cover their faces with their hands, placing the tips of their fingers on the two frontal eminences (the two bumps on the forehead in a vertical line above the pupil). This led him to develop a technique called Emotional Stress Release (see Appendix 5). People are often amazed at the power of this technique and we teach it during our 'Diagnostic Kinesiology' courses, where students often comment on how they have been helped by it.

Of importance here is to notice how this technique can remove stress instantly, and then we find that other pollutants, such as metal jewellery or washing powder, no longer cause a problem. So indeed, this can be a way to break the circle of ill health completely, but we cannot say permanently, because there will always be other stresses that spring up to take the place of the one previously removed. To use the emotional stress release technique on an ongoing basis will continue to address these stresses.

We can progress around the circle to nutrition and water. Often improvements in these areas, which have been discussed, will make a difference, but again, our bodies have been designed to cope for brief periods without food and water, and it is virtually impossible to ensure that we are never malnourished or dehydrated.

So we come to the heading of the other maintaining causes that we have discussed. If in doubt as to whether any of these are relevant, we would recommend just removing all metals for a month (jewellery, watches etc.) and degaussing three times daily, to see if there is any significant difference to your health.

Perhaps you do consider stress to be a maintaining cause of most problems, but in order to permanently break the circle we need to ask two questions. Firstly, which is the most unnatural factor, and secondly, what can we deal with easily? If the answer to these two questions is the same, then that is where we must concentrate our efforts. We will then have removed the blockage that stops the body beginning to heal itself.

In this book we may not be saying a lot that is new, but we are saying what doctors and health practitioners said 200 years ago and bringing it up to date. When Dr Samuel Hahnemann wrote, *"First remove all hurtful influences that affect the patients from without"*,[78] he was giving us the key to good health. If we follow this advice and remove the maintaining cause, then we will no longer be bailing out a boat with a hole in the bottom. This in turn will mean that complementary and alternative medicine, be it homœopathy, herbal medicine, nutrition or any other well known and proved system, will be curative in a significantly increased number of cases. Chemical drugs will no longer need to be prescribed indefinitely in order to palliate, but may be needed for a short time to do a holding operation, while the body is strengthened to throw off its own toxic load.

Using the principles discussed in this book we can remove the body's, and the brain's, toxic load, and set the individual on the road to recovery.

78 Hahnemann,S.The Chronic Diseases. B.Jain Publishers. 1996

SUMMARY

- Drink lots of good quality water
- Eat healthily
- Wear clothes of natural fibres
- Be aware of what toiletries and washing powder you use
- Avoid amalgam fillings (replace if necessary)
- Be aware of what metal jewellery and watch you wear
- Wear plastic-framed glasses rather than metal frames
- Take protective measures against geopathic and electromagnetic stress:
  - Use daylight bulbs
  - Place copper coins on computers, mattresses
  - Avoid low-energy lightbulbs
  - Degausse daily
  - Invest in an Elo-Rayex
  - Use mobile and cordless phones on loudspeaker and use for a minimal time

APPENDIX 1 – MAIN POLLUTANTS

BENZENE is a common solvent that can cause much harm. It settles in the thymus gland, affecting the immune system. The weakened immune system lets many pollutants and parasites gain a foothold into our bodies. As the thymus recovers, so our immunity returns. Many viruses that commonly cause childhood and adult diseases live in our bodies, but are held in check by a healthy immune system. As our immunity becomes impaired in different ways, then we become susceptible to the childhood, adult and auto-immune diseases. For instance, as a child we may succumb to chickenpox. The body recovers, but the virus lives on, usually causing no further harm. However with a combination of stress and benzene, that virus may erupt again, this time causing shingles, a disease that is almost never troublesome unless someone has first had chickenpox. Dr Hulda Clark has written extensively about benzene, stating that it is used for sterilising equipment and is therefore usually found in trace quantities in bottled, and even distilled, water and in bottled fruit juice.

ISOPROPYL ALCOHOL is a poisonous solvent and denaturant (altering the structure of other chemicals) found in hair-colour rinses, body rubs, hand lotions, aftershave lotions, fragrances and in much processed food. It can cause nausea, vomiting, headaches, flushes, and depression.[79] The liver can become very toxic as a result of it and it can be instrumental in the development and spread of cancer.

ACETONE, XYLENE and TOLUENE can be found in breakfast cereals, decaffeinated powders and carbonated drinks. High levels of exposure for short or long periods can cause headaches, lack of muscle coordination, dizziness, confusion, and changes in one's sense of balance. Exposure of people to high levels of xylene for short peri-

79 What Doctors Don't Tell You, 1999 Vol. 10, No.7

ods can also cause irritation of the skin, eyes, nose, and throat; difficulty in breathing; problems with the lungs; delayed reaction time; memory difficulties; stomach discomfort; and possibly changes in the liver and kidneys. It can cause unconsciousness and even death at very high levels.

WOOD ALCOHOL is found in carbonated drinks, diet drinks, herb tea blends and bottled water. The side effects of wood alcohol can be abdominal pain, shortness of breath, vomiting, convulsions and unconsciousness.

HEXANE and PENTANE are found in decaffeinated beverages and METHYLENE CHLORIDE is found in fruit juice. Hexane and pentane have been found to cause nerve and lung damage. Methylene blue may cause nausea, vomiting, diarrhoea, and gastritis.

HAXANEDIONE and TRICHLOROETHANE ETHYLENE are found in flavoured foods. These can cause irritation of the skin, eyes, mucous membranes and upper respiratory tract.

SODIUM LAURYL SULPHATE is found in shampoos, hair conditioners, toothpastes and body washes. This is a strong detergent that can cause eye irritation, permanent damage to the eyes, especially in children, skin rashes, hair loss, flaking skin and mouth ulceration. When combined with other ingredients to make sodium laureth, it can form NITROSAMINES, which are carcinogenic. It easily penetrates the skin and can lodge in the heart, liver, lungs and brain.[80]

ERYTHROSINE is a red dye that causes the release of chemical substances from the nerve cells of animals, which can cause changes in behaviour.

80 What Doctors Don't Tell You, 1999, Vol. 10, No. 7

TARTRAZINE is an orange dye used in fruit squashes and many other foods, which is known to cause allergic reactions.[81]

Crude metals also enter our bodies as industrial and domestic pollutants, such as:

COPPER, which is carcinogenic, is found in copper-bottomed kettles or copper plumbing.

LEAD and CADMIUM can be found in soldered and galvanised plumbing. Cadmium causes the blood vessels to spasm and can be instrumental in hypertension and 'smoker's legs', or intermittent claudication.

NICKEL and CHROMIUM are found in dental ware and cosmetics, jewellery, and even stainless steel utensils.

ALUMINIUM appears in food and drink cans, cooking pots, talcum powder, salts and anti-perspirants. Sour food, e.g. citrus, and fruit pudding absorbs aluminium from pots and pans before being consumed.

THALLIUM is found in mercury fillings and products sterilised with mercuric chloride, e.g. nappies, tampons etc., which in turn produce thallium pollution. It was used as rat poison, but was banned in the 1970s. It is interesting to note that we have found babies with colic and diarrhoea return to health after the brand of their nappies has been changed.

MYCOTOXIN is produced by moulds and is extremely poisonous – a tiny amount can incapacitate part of the liver for days.[82] Aflatoxin is the most common mycotoxin. It is a life-threatening toxin released from Aspergillus flavus[83].

81 'The Hyperactive Child. A Parents' Guide, Eric Taylor, p.54
82 'The Cure for all Diseases', Hulda Clark p.38
83 'S□klafræ□i. I□NÚ, Bogi Ingimarsson, p.65

It is produced by moulds that grow on quite a variety of plants, so it is found in commercial fruit juice, cereal, bread, pasta, nuts, syrup, vinegar, wine and commercial bread. Adding vitamin C to the diet can help destroy the mould and help the liver to recover quickly.

ZEAR is a mycotoxin that prevents the body from detoxifying benzene and Hulda Clark states that is found present in every AIDS sufferer. The main sources are popcorn, corn, chips and brown rice.

ERGOT is found in cereals, wholegrain bread, wine and honey. It has been shown to be especially toxic to children, as their livers are unable to detoxify it and this might explain some instances of their 'Jekyll and Hyde' behaviour. Ergot can cause seizures and 'strange feelings'.

KOJIC ACID mycotoxin appears to be responsible for wood alcohol build-up, which leads to pancreas damage, invites pancreatic fluke infestation and typically results in diabetes. It is found in potato skin and coffee.

PATULIN is the major fruit toxin, present in bruised fruits. The mould that produces it can grow in patches in the intestines, where bowel bacteria e.g. E-coli and shigella can pass through the colon wall. These are then free to spread to regions of injury, and tumours may result.

APPENDIX 2 – DIAGNOSTIC KINESIOLOGY

HOW TO MEASURE ARM STRENGTH

All of the following proceedures can be done with the patient clothed and standing or seated.

The pectoralis major clavicular muscle draws the arm upwards and towards the midline of the body. The test is made with the arm rotated so the thumb is down towards the toes and with the elbow locked, making the arm straight. Pressure is on the outside of the wrist to push the arm downwards and slightly away from the body at an angle of about 30 degrees from the vertical.

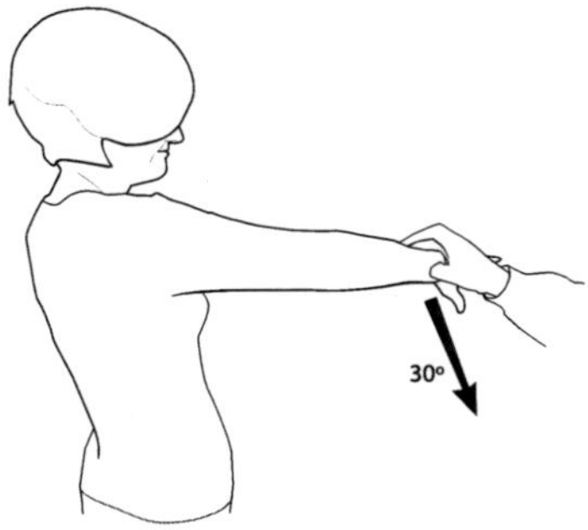

- It is essential for both people to keep breathing during the test. If either holds their breath it may confuse the test; aim to be breathing out as the pressure is applied.
- Put the limb in the exact starting position for the test.
- Indicate the direction of pressure and say, "Hold" to the person being tested.
- Pause for a fraction of a second to allow the instruction to be heard, to reach the brain and activate the muscle fibres in response to the pressure you will exert.
- Press slowly, firmly and progressively, allowing the patient to meet your pressure. If they start to push first, begin again. Use only two or three fingers until you reach optimum pressure. Maintain pressure for a second or two, then release smoothly so there is no jerkiness.

DETECTING SENSITIVITIES

1. To test whether something (e.g. coffee / mobile phone etc.) weakens the individual:
- Test arm to measure strength.
- The Practitioner holds the item to the side of the patient's face and tests again.
- If the arm being tested goes weak, this indicates that the item weakens the individual.

2. To test whether something (e.g. homœopathic remedy) strengthens the individual:
- Test arm to measure strength.
- Place magnet on pectoralis major to weaken and test again – the arm will go weak when same pressure as above is applied.
- Whilst the magnet is still held against the muscle, the practitioner holds the item on the patient's cheek near the lips and tests again.
- If the arm stays strong when an item is tested, that item strengthens the individual.

3. To test to find out which strengthening item (e.g. homœopathic remedy) is the priority at the time of testing:
- Test arm to measure strength.
- Place magnet on pectoralis major to weaken and test again – the arm will go weak when same pressure as above is applied.
- Whilst the magnet is still held against the muscle, the practitioner holds each item (individually) on the patient's cheek near the lips and tests again.
- If the arm stays strong when an item is tested, that item strengthens the individual.
- Each item that strengthens is then tested again, but this time the patient holds the middle finger in the crease of the thumb when the muscle is being tested[84].

84 Technique introduced by Alan Sales.

- Where a change occurs when the arm is tested – i.e. the arm goes weak – this is the item which the patient needs as a priority.

4. To test for an organ weakness:
- Test arm to measure strength
- Place hand over the organ to be tested and test again
  - If the arm stays strong, the organ is strong
  - If the arm goes weak, the organ is weak
- The practitioner can use their own hand or, depending on the organ, the patient can place his/her hand over the organ and the practitioner can place his/her fingers on top of the patient's hand.

5. To test whether something (e.g. homœopathic remedy) strengthens the organ:
- Test arm to measure strength
- Whilst the hand is placed over the organ, the patient holds the substance to the side of his/her face and the muscle is tested again
  - If the arm stays strong, the substance strengthens the organ
  - If the arm goes weak, the substance does not help the organ

Note: When carrying out the test for an allergic reaction, the practitioner places his/her finger:
- Over the ear to test for inherited problems
- Under the ear to test for overload of the substance.

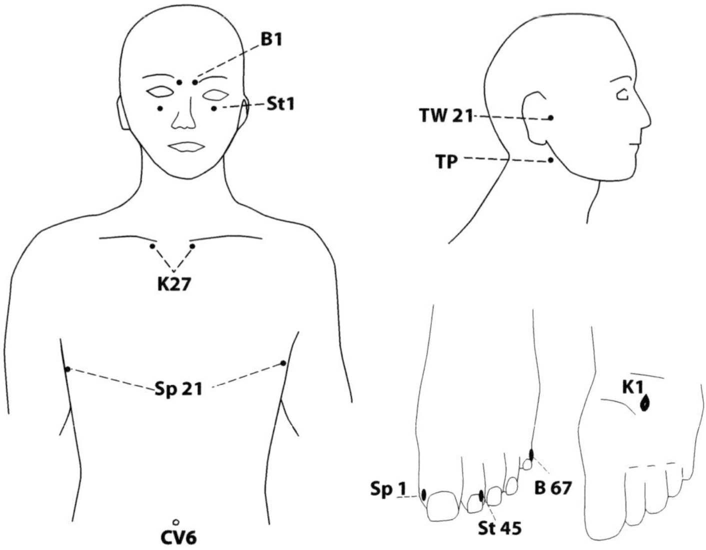

REDUCING SENSITIVITIES BY ACUPRESSURE TAPPING

Once a person has been found to be sensitive to a substance, they can be de-sensitised to it as follows:

- Stimulate the thymus by tapping anti-clockwise around it.
- Then start tapping lightly for about 20-30 seconds on 8 different location spots:
  - Bladder 1, where the inner corner of the eye meets the nose
  - Stomach 1, just underneath the eyes on top of the cheekbone
  - Kidney 27, just under where the collar bones meet the sternum
  - Spleen 21, sides of the chest underneath armpits, level with nipples
  - Spleen 1, outer edge of big toes
  - Bladder 67, outer edge of little toes
  - Stomach 45, side of second toe nearest to little toe
  - Kidney 1, medial edge of ball of big toe

These may be done in any order.

Once this 'tapping' has been completed, test the arm again whilst holding Triple Warmer (TW21) with the substance still on Central Vessel 6 (CV6) located 1cm below the navel. It should now remain strong as the person is no longer as sensitive to the substance. If it does still go weak, then the tapping needs to be repeated.

We have used this procedure on numerous occasions to desensitise people to problems related to the electrical frequency of their mobile phones, watches, and metal jewellery, as well as to pollen and foods.

OVERWHELM / LIMITED TOLERANCE PROCEDURE

We have found in our clinic that some people say that they cannot eat wheat; upon testing them we find that they do not go weak on wheat. However, if we test them for a limited tolerance to the substance they go weak. This tolerance test involves testing the muscle whilst touching a spot just underneath the jaw bone towards the ear (TP in the diagram). If they go weak on the substance whilst this spot is held it shows that although the person may not be allergic to the substance, but they can only tolerate a certain amount of it.

Tolerance can be improved by stimulating the immune system to overcome the problem. This is very similar to the previously mentioned technique.

Firstly, place the substance on CV6 and test the patient's arm whilst touching the point under their jaw line. If the muscle goes weak, this indicates a lack of tolerance to it. To test to see if the 'tap' can proceed the patient places his fingers on one of his Spleen 21 points and the practitioner holds the other Spleen 21 and muscle tests. If the arm goes weak then 'tapping' can commence. However, if the arm stays strong then it indicates that there is another priority that needs to be addressed first, such as metals, or electromagnetic stress, or that the substance is so toxic to the body that it can't accommodate an

improvement in tolerance. This would not happen with grass or pollens, but can happen with heroin or tobacco.
If the body will let us proceed, keeping the substance on CV6, firstly stimulate the thymus (tapping anti-clockwise).
There are then four places to tap:
- With the patient placing their palm over their navel with light pressure (they can do this whilst holding on to the substance), Bladder 67 and Kidney 1 are tapped.
- The patient then moves their hand from their navel to fan out over the spleen; little finger of left hand lies against bottom left rib and hand spans out over the rib cage.
- Stomach 45 and Spleen 1 are then tapped.

Muscle test again whilst touching the jaw line; if the tap is successful the arm should be strong. We have now raised the level of tolerance – it may be possible to find out how much by increasing the amount of the substance on CV6 until the muscle again unlocks. The amount of tolerance will vary depending on stress and other health factors.

If either of these 'tapping' techniques do not work, it is normally because there is another more important factor that needs to be addressed first. This diagnostic work can be complex, and may need the help of a skilled practitioner.

More on this topic can be found in Jane Thurnell-Read's book '*Energy Mismatch*', in which she talks about methods of identifying and correcting allergies, along with much more.

APPENDIX 3 – MOST DANGEROUS FUNGAL POISONS

Amanitin: A poison of the bulbous agaricus, which leads to the destruction of the liver even in small quantities, and is the most frequent cause of fungal poisoning.
Orellanin: Leads to protracted poisonings, often with permanent kidney damage.
Gyromitrin: The poison of *Gyromitra-esculenta* turban fungus that acts similarly to amanitin. What is the source of these poisons?? Particular foods??
Muscarin: Poisonous substance which is contained in many species of fungi. It acts as a nerve poison, affecting the heart and blood circulation. It can be neutralised by atropine from *Atropa belladonna*. Although it is contained in small doses in *Amanita pantherina* and *Amanita muscaria,* the real danger posed by both these fungi is due to other poisonous substances.

APPENDIX 4 – DIRECTIONS FOR PARASITE CLEANSE

Day	**Black Walnut Hull tincture** Drops once per day e.g. before a meal	**Wormwood capsules** Once per day on empty stomach (before meal)	**Clove capsules** 3 times per day, e.g. at mealtimes
1	1 drop	1	1,1,1
2	2 drops	1	2,2,2
3	3 drops	2	3,3,3
4	4 drops	2	3,3,3
5	5 drops	3	3,3,3
6	2 tsp	3	3,3,3
7		4	3,3,3
8		4	3,3,3
9	Now once a week	5	3,3,3
10		5	3,3,3
11		6	3
12		6	
13	2 tsp	7	
14		7	Now once a week
15		7	
16		7	
17		Now one a week	
18			3

After 18 days you do not need to keep a strict schedule, but instead may choose any day of the week to take all the parasite programme ingredients. Continue on the Maintenance Parasite Programme indefinitely to prevent future re-infection. (*Hulda Clark, The Cure For All Diseases*)
Black Walnut Hull tincture kills any parasite stages throughout the body.
Wormwood kills the adult intestinal flukes.
Clove kills off the parasite's eggs.

APPENDIX 5 – EMOTIONAL STRESS RELEASE TECHNIQUE

It has been proved in many cases that, by simply massaging the two frontal eminences (the two bumps on the forehead in a vertical line above the pupils), using the lightest amount of pressure whilst thinking of the most concerning aspect of the stress, the blood flow can improve as we concentrate on the problem. This allows the mind to see things in a more realistic perspective, and after having performed this 'emotional stress release' on ourselves or someone else, it becomes increasingly difficult to focus on this aspect of the problem. It seems to become less of an issue, and then we can move on to think about another aspect of the problem until that too becomes no longer the worry it originally appeared to be. It is important to focus on a single aspect of the problem whilst the lightest massage is performed for one or two minutes.

'An Introduction to Kinesiology' by Brian Butler.

APPENDIX 6 – ESSIAC TEA

Ingredients: Burdock Root; Sheeps Sorrel; Turkey Rhubarb Root; Slippery Elm.

3 times a day is recommended for people with cancer and serious ailments, twice a day for chronic complaints and once daily for maintenance and gentle detoxification.

These herbs and instructions for use can be obtained from Traditional Health, who uses only the finest of herbs and which are guaranteed free of radiation and fumigation.

APPENDIX 7 – ELO-RAYEX

The Elo-Rayex is a specially designed aerial which can reduce or eliminate the electromagnetic stress which surrounds most of us on a daily basis.

Research has shown that the human body is controlled by a number of different frequencies. Individuals who are exposed to electromagnetic frequencies emitted from PC's, electrical appliances, mobile phones, wireless internet etc, can develop physical symptoms due to their immune system being continuously compromised.

The Elo-Rayex contains 6 aerials which are exactly tuned into the main frequencies that affect the human body and absorbs them, thereby lessening their impact on the body.

A lot of people are affected by electromagnetic stress, but as it is not a visible pollutant, we are generally unaware that we are being exposed to it. Many long term health problems are caused by electromagnetic stress and in these cases the Elo-Rayex can be used to protect the individual from these harmful influences and in turn improve that person's health.

We recommend placing the Elo-Rayex on or next to the main fuse box of the house, with the writing facing upward. If you are living in a rented flat, you can attach the Elo-Rayex to the sub-distributor (fuse box). Using Kinesiology it is possible to demonstrate that the strain caused by electric smog is dramatically reduced with the use of an Elo-Rayex.

APPENDIX 8
KLAMATH BLUE-GREEN ALGAE

TYPICAL ANALYSIS OF AQUASOURCE ALGAE

KCAL Unit (100g)	375
KJ Unit (100g)	1590

GENERAL COMPOSITION %

Moisture	4.60%	Total carbohydrate	25.17%
Fat (lipids)	4.50%	Of which sugars	<0.1%
Protein	60.03%	Available carbohydrate	18.40%
Ash (Mineral material)	5.70%	Dietary fibre	7.30%

Pigments (chlorophylls and related substances) 5.10%

FATTY ACIDS COMPOSITION

Linoleic	12.39%	Palmitolinoleic	None (<0.01)
Linolenic	21.60%	Stearic	2.93%
Oleic	5.07%		
Palmitic	43.36%	Total steroidal lipids	None (<0.1)
Palmitoleic	9.80%	Cholesterol	None (<0.1)

VITAMIN COMPOSITION PER GRAM

Ascorbic Acid (C)	89.7mg	Beta Carotene	298mg
Vitamin B12 Total	8.4mcg	Vitamin B6	19.3mcg
Vitamin B1	3.7mcg	Vitamin B2	91.2mcg
Folic Acid	1.33mcg	Vitamin E	2.8IU
Vitamin B5	9.8mg	Niacin	0.8mcg

ESSENTIAL AMINO ACIDS PER GRAM

Isoleucine	29.3mg	Phenylalanine	25.9mg
Leucine	52.8mg	Threonine	32.6mg
Lysine	35.1mg	Tryptophan	6.9mg
Methionine	7.3mg	Valine	33.7mg

NON-ESSENTIAL AMINO ACIDS PER GRAM

Alanine	47.1mg	Glutamic Acid	3.8mg
Arginine	38.3mg	Glycine	30.6mg
Asparagine	45.2mg	Histidine	8.7mg
Aspartic Acid	7.3mg	Proline	30.2mg
Cystine	2.2mg	Serine	29.5mg
Glutamine	77.1mg	Tyrosine	19.6mg

MINERAL CONTENT PER GRAM

Boron	11.2mg	Molybdenum	4.8mcg
Calcium	33mg	Nickel	3.2mcg
Chloride	777mcg	Phosphate (Total)	5.8mg
Cobalt	2.1mcg	Potassium	16.2mg
Copper	6.9mcg	Selenium	0.21mcg
Chromium	0.17mcg	Silicon	0.15mg
Fluoride	41.2mcg	Sodium	2.4mg
Germanium	0.18mcg	Tin	$<$0.1mcg
Iodine complexes	0.98mcg	Titanium	16.3mcg
Iron	34.2mg	Vanadium	1.3mcg
Manganese	26.1mcg	Zinc	22.6mcg
Magnesium	2mg		

Aphanizomenon Flos-Aquae, fresh dried and never frozen.
Analysis completed by Microsearch Laboratories Ltd.

CONTACTS & SOURCES

For further information please contact:
Newlands Park Healthcare Centre,
48 Newlands Park, London SE26 5NE
Tel: 020 8659 5001
e-mail: dropbox@traditional-health.co.uk
www.traditional-health.co.uk
www.allergytestinglondon.co.uk

UK
Most products mentioned in this book can be obtained from Newlands Park Healthcare Centre.

APPENDIX 9 – THE METAL IN YOUR MOUTH

by Dr K. Hajikakou Bsc, BDS, LDS, RCS(Eng), DIHom, LFHom (Dent), Dip Clin Hypnosis, PGCE

INTRODUCTION

This article looks at the effects of dental materials on the health of the individual. There are many dental materials in use to restore broken teeth. The main criteria considered by the dental materials experts have been their physical characteristics, e.g. coefficients of expansion and contraction, compressive and shear strengths. Little, if any, thought has been given to the biological effects of these materials. In particular it now appears that metals used to restore teeth can have profound effects on the physical, mental and spiritual health of patients. Present day non-metal or white filling materials, i.e. composites and porcelains appear, at present, to be safer alternatives.

Broadening the field of dental toxicity would include some things that I cannot go into here, such as dental hygiene products, e.g. toothpaste, antiseptic mouthwashes, impression materials, rubber products and acrylate resins used in dentures and root canal medications. The effects of ionising radiation from dental x-ray machines could also be included, not to mention fluoride, which calcifies the pineal gland, accumulates in the pituitary and has a marked hypothyroid action! It is no wonder that Professor Vimy (Professor of Oral Medicine, Calgary University, Canada), referring to the dental profession, said "Never has so much harm been done to so many by so few" (Vimy, 2000).

METALS USED IN CROWNS (CAPS)

Gold is becoming more popular with many dentists in this country. Dental gold is an alloy made of gold, silver, copper, palladium, platinum and zinc. The following metals are to be found in dental casting alloys used to make crowns and bridges: beryllium, cobalt, cadmium, gallium, nickel, rhodium, iridium and indium. Unfortunately, these alloys release metal ions into the body.

Is there any evidence that metal ions can cause harm? According to Professor John Wataha (Professor of Oral Rehabilitation at the Medical College of Georgia, Augusta, USA), the answer is a resounding yes. In sufficient concentrations and in certain forms metal ions can kill tissues, cause allergies, inflammatory reactions and cancer (Wataha, 1999).

Swelling and irritation with redness and pain in the region of a metal crown could well signify an allergic reaction to one or more of the metals. Dermatitis having a perioral distribution (around the mouth) is also suggestive of allergy originating from a dental source. Palladium and nickel are highly allergenic metals.

AMALGAM FILLINGS

Before considering the effects of mercury, let us look at the electrical activity of amalgam fillings. Each filling acts like a battery (Certosimo, 1996). As the filling is an alloy and is bathed by an electrolyte, i.e. saliva, a potential difference arises leading to electrical currents being generated. These currents are of an order of magnitude 1,000 times greater than those generated by nerve cells. This can lead to the impairment of nerve functioning and neurotransmitter release (Sheppard, 1997). The proximity of the brain to oral amalgam fillings can, in some patients, lead to neurological problems such as "brain fog" (the inability to think clearly, and depression). From my clinical experience patients have reported being "clear-headed", as if a fog has lifted, after having had their amalgam fillings removed. This effect is experienced rapidly, whereas mercury toxicity effects take longer to resolve.

WHEN IS A POISON NOT A POISON?

The answer to this riddle is, of course, when it is in your mouth! Amalgam (a mixture of mercury with another metal) or "silver" fillings contain silver, copper, tin, zinc and mercury. Amalgam fillings are made up of 50% mercury and should be known as mercury fillings, not silver fillings.

It is ironic that waste amalgam (i.e. outside the body) must be stored in secure conditions owing to the release of mercury vapour and has to be disposed of by licensed disposal companies. However, when it is placed in people's teeth it "miraculously" transforms itself into a complete inert material, which is perfectly safe! At least that is the official line. "It is generally agreed that if amalgam was introduced today as a restorative material, it would never pass FDA (Food and Drug Administration) approval" (Wolfe et al, 1983). The case against using amalgam is, in my opinion, overwhelming.

AMALGAM — SOME FACTS

When I was studying dentistry I was told that mercury was "locked into" the filling and, therefore, was not released. This is totally untrue (Jones et al, 1983). Mercury vapour is released during the entire life of the filling. As mercury vapour is colourless, odourless and tasteless it escapes undetected by the recipient of that filling. More vapour is released each time your chew, drink anything hot or brush your teeth. The more fillings you have, the larger the surface area of the fillings the more vapour you will be exposed to, and the greater the health risk. The vapour is rapidly absorbed via the lungs and nasal mucosa and accumulates in areas of high metabolic activity, e.g. brain, gut, kidneys, liver and heart. The toxicity of mercury is well documented: it is more toxic than lead and arsenic combined. The toxic threshold, i.e. the level below which it is considered safe has never been established. The World Health Organisation states "No level of exposure to mercury can be considered harmless". WHO also states that dental amalgam is the single largest source of mercury exposure for the public, contributing upto 84% of daily intake:

- mercury from fillings (average of 8) 17 mcg/day
- mercury from all other sources: seafood, air and water 2-6 mcg/day (WHO, 1991)

Autopsy studies confirm that the brain is the critical target organ for mercury. Brain tissue mercury levels are far higher in patients with amalgam fillings than in the patients having no fillings present. Professor Boyd Haley (Professor of Biochemistry at the University of Kentucky, USA) has demonstrated the effects mercury has on brain biochemistry. Structures known as microtubules found in nerve cells,w which are essential for transportation of substances along the nerve are greatly affected by the presence of mercury. This may be a key contributory factor in Alzheimer's disease. Haley has also demonstrated hat in the presence of cadmium, another widely present pollutant, mercury toxicity is greatly increased. Mercury is found in structures associated with memory, e.g. the hippocampus, amygdala and nucleus basalis.

Experiments in sheep and monkeys clearly show that when mercury fillings are place, the mercury deposits in the brain, kidneys and liver. Kidney function determined by albumin excretion (albumin is a normal blood protein) is greatly reduced in those animals receiving amalgam fillings (Vimy et al, 1990). Another worrying fact is that mercury crosses over the placenta into the foetus within two days of amalgam placement, accumulating in the fetal brain and liver (Vimy et al, 1990). Breast milk has also been found to contain significant levels of mercury.

Oral and gut bacteria can metabolise inorganic mercury to organic mercury, e.g. methyl mercury, another powerful toxin. And if this is not bad enough the presence of mercury has been shown to increase the resistance of oral and gut bacteria to antibiotics within two weeks of amalgam placement (Summers et al, 1993). Ampicillin, tetracyclin, streptomycin, erythromycin, kanamycin and chloramphenicol are all antibiotics whose effects are greatly reduced in the presence of mercury.

Oral lichen planus, a condition where the oral mucosa changes to form white patches with a lacy pattern has now a well-established link with mercury containing amalgam fillings. This is seen in those individuals who have sensitivity to mercury and where amalgam filling is in direct contact with the oral tissue. Is this a hazard to health professionals who deal with amalgam fillings?

Dentists have four times more mercury in the urine compared with the rest of the population and a suicide rate two to six times greater than average. Is this due to a stressful job or is it, perhaps, mercury related? I feel it is the latter. Female dental personnel have twice the rate of infertility, miscarriage and spontaneous abortion compared to the rest of the female population.

The earliest symptoms of long-term, low-level mercury poisoning are extremely subtle and easily misdiagnosed. Certain idiosyncrasies may develop or subtle psychiatric, neurological problems may begin to show. Mercury from dental amalgam does, in my opinion, constitute a significant health hazard. Controlled scientific studies looking at the effects on the health of patients of mercury from dental amalgam fillings have never been conducted. The scientific experts say that there is no evidence to show that mercury from amalgam does any harm. Does this, therefore, mean it is safe? I think not. Bertand Russell, the philosopher, once said "Even when all the experts agree, they may well be wrong".

SYMPTOMS OF MERCURY TOXICITY

ACUTE

metallic taste - due to electrical activity and corrosion
burning pains - mouth, throat and stomach
increased salivation
swollen salivatory glands
abdominal pains
diarrhoea and vomiting

CHRONIC

Nervous system

irritability
anxiety/nervousness, often with difficulty in breathing
restlessness
exaggerated response to stimulation
fearfulness
lack of self-control
fits of anger, with violent irrational behaviour
loss of self-confidence
indecision
shyness or timidity, being easily embarrassed
loss of memory
inability to concentrate
lethargy/drowsiness
insomnia
mental depression, despondency
withdrawal
suicidal tendencies
manic depression
numbness and tingling of the hands, feet, fingers, toes and lips
muscle weakness progressing to paralysis
ataxia
tremors/trembling of hands, feet, lips, eyelids or tongue
incoordination
myoneural transmission failure resembling myasthenia gravis
motor neurone disease
multiple sclerosis

Oral disorders

bleeding gums
alveolar bone loss
loosening of teeth
excessive salivation
foul breath
metallic taste
burning sensation, with tingling of lips and face
tissue pigmentation (amalgam tattoo of gums)
leukoplakia
ulceration of gingiva, palate and tongue

Gastro-intestinal

food sensitivities, especially to milk and eggs
abdominal cramps, colitis, diverticulitis or other GI complaints
chronic diarrhoea/constipation

Systemic effects

chronic headaches
allergies
severe dermatitis
unexplained reactivity
thyroid disturbance
subnormal body temperature
cold, clammy skin, especially hands and feet
excessive perspiration, with frequent night sweats
unexplained sensory symptoms, including pain
unexplained numbness or burning sensations

REFERENCES (FOR THE METAL IN YOUR MOUTH)

Certosimo, A.J. and O'Connor, R.P. (1996) "Oral electricity", General Dentistry, July/August: 324-326

Conference of IAOMT (International Academy of Oral Medicine and Toxicology) Oxford, June, 2000

Hansen, K. et al (1984) "A survey of metal induced mutagen in vitro and in vivo", Journal American Coll. Toxicology, 3: 381-430

Jones, D.W. et al (1983) "Mercury leaves dental amalgam continuously throughout the lifetime of the filling", Canadian Dental Association Journal, 4906: 378-395

Sheppard, A.R. and Eisentod, M. (1997) Biological Effects of Electric and Magnetic Fields in Extremely Low Frequency, New York: New York University Press

Summers, A.O. et al (1993) "Mercury released from dental 'silver' fillings provokes an increase in mercury and antibiotic resistant bacteria in oral and intestinal floras of primates", Antimicrobial Agents and Chemotherapy, April: 301-323

Vimy, M.J. et al (1990) "Maternal fetal distribution of mercury released from dental amalgam fillings", The American Physiological Society, R939-R945

Vimy, M.J. et al (1990) "Whole-body imaging of the distribution of mercury released from dental fillings into monkey tissues", FASEB Journal, Vol.4: 3256-3260

Wataha, J. (1999) "Biocompatability of dental alloys", The Probe, March: 21-32

World Health Organisation Criteria, 1991:118, Geneva, Switzerland

FURTHER READING (FOR THE METAL IN YOUR MOUTH)

Huggins, H. (1993) It's all in your head: the link between mercury amalgam and illness. New York: Avery Publishing Group Inc.

PROTOCOL FOR SAFE REMOVAL OF AMALGAM FILLINGS

There are many protocol regimes to aid mercury elimination during and after amalgam removal. The cost of supplements and the complexities of taking certain products can be a major barrier for some patients. I suggest a fairly simple regime with costs kept at a reasonable level:

- before amalgam removal: Mercurius solubilis 30c or Amalagam 30c, 2 doses a day for one or two days before treatment
- after amalgam removal: one dose of Mercury solubilis 30c immediately after treatment.

Sulphur naturally binds free mercury and thus aids its elimination. Foods rich in sulphur should be eaten plentiful and as often as possible for at least one week post-amalgam removal. Such foods are onions, garlic, eggs (yolk), pulses and brassicas, e.g. sprouts, cabbage and broccoli. A selenium supplement with vitamins A, C and E is beneficial taken for one week after removal. The patient should drink plenty of good quality water.

It should be noted that amalgam fillings must be removed in a set sequence depending upon their electrical activity. In each quadrant of the mouth the filling having the highest negative charge should be removed first and so on. Remove the fillings in descending order of negative charge, until a filling with a positive reading is reached. If such a filling is present it would be removed but only after the negative charged fillings have gone.

It is essential that amalgam fillings are removed using a rubber dam and high volume suction. I think it sensible that patients should use a dentist committed to amalgam free dentistry with experience of amalgam removal and composite placement. A dentist still using amalgam might not have the experience necessary to undertake this procedure to ensure the best outcome for the patient. Patients are sometimes told that composite is not strong enough, long lasting enough or suitable for large fillings. My experience has taught me that this is completely untrue. In 15 years in practice I have never yet had to replace a composite filling which has failed and some have been very large.

There are two ways of tackling amalgam removal. One is (as I would term it) "kill or cure", whereby all amalgam fillings are removed within one week. The other method I call a "softly softly" approach whereby amalgam fillings are removed one by one at intervals of at least four weeks. This has the advantage of allowing the body to recover between each "assault on the system", which is how I imagine the body perceives the process and to which it would react accordingly. I favour the latter method as being gentler and kinder for the patient.

Because of the time and expense involved I recommend that amalgam removal should only be undertaken as a last resort once the patient's practitioner has exhausted all other avenues towards the patient recovery.

Once all amalgams have been removed it is important that no more mercury enters the body as this would defeat the detoxification process. Fish should not be eaten while there is still evidence of mercury toxicity, possibly indefinitely. Patients should take saunas regularly for several months as this encourages waste products, including mercury, to be eliminated via the skin.

Finally, the two most powerful natural products for mobilising and eliminating stored mercury from body tissues are Cilantro (Chinese parsley) and Chlorella (green algae). Cilantro is taken as drops (orally) or rubbed into the wrists or ankles. Chlorella tablets are taken orally in an ascending dosage scheme to suit the patient, starting at 1g three times daily for one week only. Initially, careful supervision is necessary.

Dr K. Hajikakou Bsc BDS LDS RCS(Eng) DIHom LFHom (Dent) Dip Clin Hypnosis PGCE
Dr Hajikakou runs a homœopathic amalgam free practice at Rye, East Sussex.

Index